Let Them Eat Dirt

D1708002

Let Them Eat Dirt

Homemade Baby Food to
Nourish Your Family

Andrea Bemis

creator of Dishing Up the Dirt

PAGE STREET
PUBLISHING CO.

PAGE STREET
PUBLISHING CO.

Copyright © 2023 Andrea Bemis

First published in 2023 by
Page Street Publishing Co.
27 Congress Street, Suite 1511
Salem, MA 01970
www.pagestreetpublishing.com

All rights reserved. No part of this book may be reproduced or used, in any form or by any means, electronic or mechanical, without prior permission in writing from the publisher.

Distributed by Macmillan, sales in Canada by The Canadian Manda Group.

27   26   25   24   23   1   2   3   4   5

ISBN-13: 978-1-64567-960-8
ISBN-10: 1-64567-960-8

Library of Congress Control Number: 2022947124

Cover and book design by Meg Baskis for Page Street Publishing Co.
Food photography by Andrea Bemis. Cover photo and lifestyle photography by Kelly Turso.

Printed and bound in the United States

Page Street Publishing protects our planet by donating to nonprofits like The Trustees, which focuses on local land conservation.

To the absolute loves of my life—Pepper and Maize. You have captured my heart and given me my passion. Thank you for living this crazy, beautiful and dirty life with me. Love, mama.

Contents

Introduction

The result of my parenting journey thus far is this book. It chronicles how I began feeding my children the same farm-fresh ingredients I've long written about as an organic vegetable farmer and cookbook author. This book is not meant to be a guide to pediatric nutrition, or a meal plan to follow. Instead, it's a look at my evolving approach to feeding my family. This book is part cookbook, and part love letter to my daughters, who are my inspiration for keeping my head held high and the reason I advocate for real food, grown on real dirt, by real people.

Whether you're here because you're starting solids for the first time with your baby or you're looking for fresh, nourishing and new ideas for simple snacks, family dinner or Sunday brunch, this book is for you. I hope these pages inspire you to start new traditions with your family, including taking a playful approach to trying different tastes and textures, while also giving you an easy-to-follow guide for supplying good nutrition through kid-friendly meals.

One of the developmental milestones I most looked forward to with my oldest daughter, Pepper, was the introduction of solid foods to her diet. As a farmer, food writer and new mother, I had visions of her frolicking in the fields and eating homegrown produce alongside me and my husband, Taylor. Instead, our first attempt at solids had both Pepper and myself in tears—her from severe constipation and me from worry that feeding her rice cereal was my first major parenting mistake.

One morning soon after the rice cereal incident, I read an Instagram story by Dr. Mark Hyman that stopped me in my tracks. He wrote, "Our children's taste buds have been hijacked by the food industry and they are paying the ultimate price." As a new mom, starting to feed my little one solid foods for the very first time, this statement terrified me. It also led me down a rabbit hole of researching childhood nutrition, disease and just how you're supposed to feed a brand-new eater.

I discovered that the rapid rise in childhood obesity, diabetes, cancer, fatty liver disease, attention-deficit/hyperactivity disorder, depression, anxiety and other behavioral problems are no coincidence. Young children and families are constantly exposed to harmful commercial marketing, typically seeing tens of thousands of advertisements a year for addictive substances and unhealthy commodities such as fast food, sugar-sweetened beverages, convenience snacks and even packaged and highly processed "health" foods, which all contribute to obesity and chronic diseases in young children. Babies under the age of 2 are especially susceptible, as their food preferences are being developed and their fragile digestive systems and gut microbiome are forming. Unfortunately, the food and beverage industry has used this knowledge to their advantage and have duped parents into believing that certain foods and drinks are essential for health and development. The truth is, most of these foods are designed to be addictive and are not a natural way of feeding children.

The Baby Food "FACTS" report from the UConn Rudd Center for Food Policy and Health found only 4 out of 80 baby and toddler snacks met nutritious standards. Additionally, 50 percent of baby food snacks and 83 percent of toddler food snacks contained added sweeteners. We're truly training our children to prefer sugary foods from the very beginning, and big corporations are profiting.

As a new, vulnerable mom navigating through the different stages of feeding my young family, I have fallen victim to some of the false advertising from the food industry and the doctors promoting it. I steered off my own track and ignored my gut several times in the early stages of feeding my baby but have come full circle and feel honored to share my experience with you.

In addition to sharing recipes that are sorted by ages and stages, in this book you'll find some of the tips and tricks I discovered along the way. These include the importance of eating together with your baby or child—because no one likes eating alone, or worse, to be stared at while they eat alone, even young babies!—as well as why it's good to eat the same foods as your children (if you want your kids to like kale, they need to see you eating kale!). You'll also find reminders to encourage toddlers to help chop, whisk and crack an egg for home-cooked meals, plus some of my go-to kitchen gadgets and a "little remedies" section to help soothe basic illness. I've also included a write-up dedicated to the biggest lesson learned of all—the mindset shift required when cooking for an infant became cooking with a toddler. (HINT: Forget about having a picture-perfect kitchen!)

Although most kids go through "picky eater" stages as a natural part of development, the fact that Pepper eats most everything we put in front of her—from Pumpkin Chili (page 101) to Veggie-Loaded Turkey Bites (page 79)—gives me hope that as she gets a little older, our family will continue to enjoy eating the same meals together. Because honestly, making separate "kid" dinners each night sounds exhausting.

I never thought cooking for a toddler would become a true passion of mine, but I'd be lying if I said I haven't had fun creating simple recipes using fresh, seasonal ingredients while trying to win over my toughest critic to date—never before have I had anyone reject my food by looking me straight in the eye while throwing a plate of lovingly prepared food straight on the ground!

I hope that you and your family find the same joy as you create new memories in the kitchen with recipes that you hopefully turn to time and time again for years to come.

—Andrea

How to Use This Book

Cooking with whole foods simply means choosing foods that are in their natural state or as close to it as possible. The recipes in this book utilize whole fruits, vegetables, meat, fish, sprouted grains, whole-milk dairy, legumes, nuts and seeds. These are the fundamental ingredients that help babies and young children thrive. The recipes also include nourishing fats in the form of grass-fed butter, ghee, duck fat, coconut oil, beef tallow and extra virgin olive oil. Babies and young children need a lot of healthy fats to help their brains and little bodies grow. You can use most of these fats interchangeably throughout the book, so work with what's available to you.

I know what you may be thinking: Whole foods sound great but cooking from scratch with a newborn or toddler sounds impossible. I hear you! Since becoming a parent, it really does feel like everything has changed. I love a slow and thoughtful approach to food, but the reality is that I don't have the time I used to, and it seems every other parent I know is in the same boat.

To try and meet you where you are—which, if you're like me, is the intersection of good intentions and a shortage of time—I've organized this book a little differently from my last two cookbooks. My hope is that this format will be a good fit for anyone who, like me, hopes they'll open a book up to exactly what they need.

Let Them Eat Dirt is divided into three sections: first foods, getting the hang of solids and family favorites. Each section of the book has a short introduction with tips and tricks as well as research and information on the fundamentals of feeding babies, young children and whole families. If you're just starting solids, you'll want to start at the beginning; if you have a toddler or older kids, you can jump between the second and third sections, as they are aimed toward everyone (from 8 months through 100 years old!).

I know this season of life is busy for all of you parents out there. Navigating exciting milestones, unsettling statistics and busy schedules, while trying to find some joy can feel overwhelming. But I truly hope this book can offer some relief or at least a little inspiration. Because when it comes right down to it, the most important thing (for me at least) is to find some joy at the dinner table and connect with my family through a home-cooked meal.

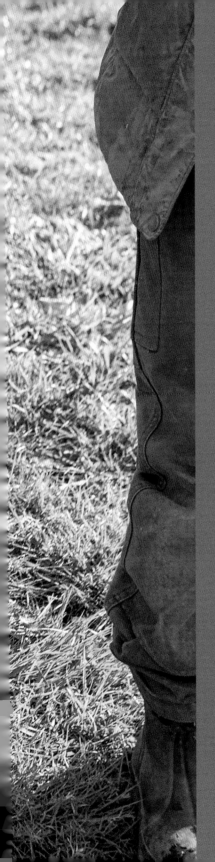

Part I:

First Foods
(6–8 months)

The "What & When" for Starting Solids

Before we dig in, let's set some realistic expectations about introducing solids to your child, and mealtimes with kids in general. The process isn't always straightforward, and what was loved one day may be refused the next. So starting solids is a good opportunity to harness some humor and practice patience and grace, because the reward—eating nutritious meals as a family—will be worth the trouble.

The common guidance from pediatricians is that kids are often ready to begin eating and digesting solid foods at around 6 months. The reasoning behind this timing takes into account a few important factors, balancing the development of a child's digestive system—which is why doctors don't advise starting solids much sooner—with a child's need for an array of vitamins and minerals as they grow.

The idea is not to go from breast milk or formula straight to solid-only meals, but rather to introduce food alongside breast milk or formula and then eventually begin to rely more on solids for sustenance and less on liquids. And don't get discouraged if your baby isn't eating much or turns their nose up at broccoli. Rest assured they are getting most of their nutritional needs met with milk.

Food for Thought: It can take a baby or toddler up to 30 exposures to a particular food before they accept it. Continue offering the foods you want your child to eat, even if they don't touch it. The more times they see a food the more familiar they'll become and eventually surprise you! You can also try serving a food a few different ways to mix it up. As a rule of thumb, have the same foods on your plate so they see you enjoying it too.

Beef
& Carrot
(page 32)

Deviled
Cauliflower
Mash
(page 22)

Prune Puree
(page 152)

Simple Pees
& Butter
(page 21)

Peaches
& Cream
(page 30)

Coconut
Beets
(page 24)

Chicken
Liver Pate
(page 34)

Cinnamon
Spice Squash
(page 23)

If I can give any guidance, based on my own experience, it's to give yourself plenty of grace. Although it can sometimes feel like it, there is no race to see whose baby ate avocado first, or which child was the quickest at developing a taste for curry. By introducing tiny portions, then waiting for a reaction—both to the taste in the mouth and later texture, as their precious body develops familiarity with new foods and learns to digest them—you'll help them ease into this big new world of taste and texture.

Food for Thought: I learned this the hard way, but try and have the food you are going to serve your baby ready right away. They have a short attention span and, if the food isn't within reach, they may get restless in their high chair and lose interest before the food is even ready!

Simple Peas & Butter

Yield: ¼ cup (60 ml)

This is one of those simple concoctions that tastes so darn delicious, you'll find yourself making this often for yourself, even after your baby surpasses purees. We still make this every spring when fresh peas are available at our farm, and I love spreading this puree on sourdough toast and sprinkling it with fresh chives, olive oil and a fat pinch of fine sea salt.

½ cup (73 g) fresh shelled or frozen thawed peas

2 tsp (9 g) unsalted butter or ghee

1 tsp minced fresh dill or mint (optional)

Bone broth or water to thin, as needed

Blanch the peas in boiling water until bright green and crisp tender, about 5 minutes for fresh peas and 2 to 3 minutes for frozen peas (don't overcook the peas; if they cook for too long, they lose nutrients—you want to pull them from the water right after they turn bright green). Immediately rinse under cold water. Add the drained peas to the bowl of a food processor or blender (or use an immersion blender), then add the butter and herbs (if using), and process until smooth, adding just a touch of bone broth or water to thin as needed.

For your beginner eater, serve about 1 tablespoon (15 ml) on a spoon and feed your little one, or let them practice guiding this to their mouth on their own. You can also simply let them use their hands and get a little messy and scoop up fistfuls.

Store in a sealed glass container in the fridge for up to 4 days or freeze for up to 3 months.

Variation: Try this same combination with green beans!

Food for Thought: Fat-soluble vitamins (A, D, E & K) will absorb better when consumed with a nourishing fat. All the purees in this book include healthy fats to make them more nutritious. Feel free to use whatever fat you prefer. We love the health benefits of ghee, grass-fed butter, duck fat, coconut oil, olive oil or beef tallow.

Deviled Cauliflower Mash

Yield: 1 cup (240 ml)

This is a wonderful, nutrient-dense recipe for your baby. The secret ingredient is a simple hard-boiled egg yolk, which is rich in omega-3 fatty acids and in the good cholesterol needed for brain development. I usually roast a whole head of cauliflower when I'm making this and use what I need for this recipe then save the rest for nibbling on myself (though I'll admit this recipe tastes really darn good as a puree and I often dip carrot sticks in it for a tasty snack).

2 cups (200 g) diced cauliflower florets

2 tbsp (30 ml) melted ghee, duck fat or olive oil

1 hard-boiled egg yolk

1 tbsp (14 g) unsalted butter

¼ cup (60 ml) plain whole-milk yogurt (goat or cow) + more to thin as needed (can substitute bone broth or water too)

½ tsp dried thyme

Preheat the oven to 350°F (175°C). Toss the cauliflower with the cooking fat and place on a rimmed baking sheet. Place in the oven and roast until the cauliflower is fork tender and lightly browned (but not charred), about 30 minutes. Remove from the oven.

Place the cauliflower in the bowl of a food processor or high-speed blender with the hard-boiled egg yolk, butter, yogurt and thyme. Process until completely smooth. If the texture is too thick, add a touch of bone broth, water or more yogurt to thin as needed. Taste and adjust seasonings as needed.

For your beginner eater, serve about 1 tablespoon (15 ml) on a spoon and feed your little one, or let them practice guiding this to their mouth on their own. You can also simply let them use their hands and get a little messy and scoop up fistfuls.

Store in an airtight glass container in the fridge for up to 4 days or freezer for up to 3 months.

Variations: Use this same recipe but swap the cauliflower for turnips, kohlrabi or sweet potatoes.

Cinnamon Spice Squash

Yield: ½ cup (120 ml)

This is a great recipe to make during the winter months. It's naturally sweet thanks to ripe winter squash and, with the addition of butter and cinnamon, it tastes like a sweet treat. When I was first making this for Pepper, I would enjoy mine right along with her, but I'd stir the puree into my morning cup of oatmeal.

1 heaping cup (150 g) diced winter squash (pumpkin, butternut, kabocha or Hubbard)

1½ tbsp (23 ml) melted ghee, butter, or coconut oil

1 tsp cinnamon

Heat the oven to 375°F (190°C). Toss the squash with the melted cooking fat and spread on a rimmed baking sheet. Place in the oven and roast until just fork tender and lightly golden brown, about 30 minutes, tossing the squash halfway through the cook time.

Remove the squash from the oven and let it cool for 15 minutes. Use an immersion blender, food processor or high-speed blender to puree the squash to your desired consistency along with the cinnamon. If the mixture seems too thick, add a touch of water or plain whole-milk yogurt (for added probiotics) to thin as needed.

For your beginner eater, serve about 1 tablespoon (15 ml) on a spoon and feed your little one, or let them practice guiding this to their mouth on their own. You can also simply let them use their hands and get a little messy and scoop up fistfuls.

Store in an airtight glass container in the fridge for up to 4 days or freezer for up to 3 months.

Variations: Try this same combination with sweet potatoes or yams.

Food for Thought: Learning to eat isn't just about nutrition; it's a sensory experience, and letting your baby play with a spoon that has some food on it is also a great way to practice fine motor skills. If the food eventually makes it to your baby's mouth, bonus!

Coconut Beets

Yield: ½ cup (120 ml)

This is a fun and different way to enjoy beets. Introducing beets early on is a great way to get your kiddos' taste buds set up to enjoy more "earthy" flavors. Not only that, but beets are chock full of important nutrients to help your little one grow. They are rich in folate, manganese and copper, which are all essential for growth and development. Don't be alarmed if your baby's poop or pee turns red or pink after consuming beets! It's totally normal! I love spreading this puree onto a piece of sourdough toast and drizzling a little honey and flakey sea salt for a tasty snack for myself.

1 tbsp (15 ml) coconut oil

1 medium-sized beet, washed and cut into small dice (no need to peel)

2 tbsp (30 ml) full-fat coconut cream (see Note)

Heat the coconut oil in a skillet over medium heat. Add the diced beets and cook, stirring occasionally, until softened, about 15 minutes.

Place the cooked beets and coconut cream in the bowl of a food processor or blender and puree until smooth. Add a touch of water to thin as needed.

For your beginner eater, serve about 1 tablespoon (15 ml) on a spoon and feed your little one, or let them practice guiding this to their mouth on their own. You can also simply let them use their hands and get a little messy and scoop up fistfuls.

Store in an airtight glass container in the fridge for up to 4 days or freezer for up to 3 months.

Variations: Try with carrots or sweet potatoes.

Note: To avoid serving young babies foods that come from a can (even BPA-free cans contain harmful chemicals), I like to make coconut cream by blending equal parts coconut butter (which you can purchase in a glass jar) with hot water in a blender. Store in the fridge for up to 7 days.

Steamed Apples & Cinnamon

Yield: ½ cup (120 ml)

This is a lovely first food to serve to a baby. Not only is this a breeze to whip up, but it's a delicious, comforting puree that tastes great served slightly warm and eaten straight up with a spoon (adults and babies alike!). This is a great recipe to turn to as your baby gets older because it can be stirred into oatmeal, yogurt or cottage cheese. The butter is used here to help balance the sugar carbohydrates but also adds a lovely flavor. Feel free to use coconut oil or ghee for a dairy-free version.

1 medium-sized apple, peeled, cored and chopped

3 tbsp (45 ml) water

1 tbsp (14 g) unsalted butter

¼ tsp ground cinnamon

Place the apple in a saucepan with the water and butter. Bring to a simmer and cook until the apple is fork tender, 15 to 20 minutes. Add more water to the pan if necessary.

Remove the pan from the heat and add the contents to a high-speed blender or food processor, along with the cinnamon. Process until smooth.

For your beginner eater, serve about 1 tablespoon (15 ml) on a spoon and feed your little one, or let them practice guiding this to their mouth on their own. You can also simply let them use their hands and get a little messy and scoop up fistfuls.

Store in an airtight glass container in the fridge for up to 4 days or freezer for up to 3 months.

Variation: Try this with pears!

Stewed Berries & Yogurt

Yield: ¼ cup (60 ml)

I love stewed berries, and so does Pepper. Even as a toddler, Pepper still requests stewed berries for breakfast to add to her oatmeal or Greek yogurt bowls. There's something really comforting about warm, jammy berries that we adore. Not only that, but berries are a great introductory food because they are chock full of antioxidants, which help fight free radicals in the body. We serve these with a little butter to help balance the sugar carbohydrates. Feel free to use another nourishing fat like coconut oil or ghee.

½ cup (80 g) mixed frozen berries (such as blueberries, blackberries, raspberries and cherries)

3 tbsp (45 ml) water

1 tbsp (14 g) unsalted butter

Pinch of ground ginger

3 tbsp (45 ml) plain whole-milk yogurt (cow, goat or sheep)

Combine the berries, water, butter and ginger in a saucepan over medium-high heat. Simmer until the berries thicken, 10 to 15 minutes. Remove the pan from the heat and use an immersion blender to blend the berries to your desired consistency. Mix with the yogurt and serve.

For your beginner eater, serve about 1 tablespoon (15 ml) on a spoon and feed your little one, or let them practice guiding this to their mouth on their own. You can also simply let them use their hands and get a little messy and scoop up fistfuls.

Store in an airtight glass container in the fridge for up to 4 days or the freezer for up to 3 months.

Variations: This works well with stewed apples, peaches or pears.

Salmon & Sauerkraut

Yield: ¼ cup (60 ml)

The list of health benefits from salmon is long! But I will keep this short. Salmon is a wonderful first food to start your growing baby with. It is chock full of brain-boosting omega-3 fatty acids, B vitamins and plenty of protein, to name just a few of its benefits. Paired with probiotic-rich sauerkraut, this is a lovely little "meal" I can get behind. A quick note: Sauerkraut tends to be naturally high in sodium. We rinse it for this recipe to remove some of the salt but, because of the health benefits of sauerkraut, I believe it's worth getting your little one used to the strong flavor early on. These days, Pepper will eat a forkful right out of the sauerkraut jar!

⅓ cup (80 g) cooked salmon, flaked

1 tbsp (15 ml) plain whole-milk yogurt (sheep, goat or cow)

1 tsp sauerkraut, rinsed under cold water to remove some of the salt and drained

Bone broth or water to thin as needed

Place the cooked salmon, yogurt and sauerkraut in a food processor and pulse until smooth. Add bone broth or water to thin as needed.

For your beginner eater, serve about 1 tablespoon (15 ml) on a spoon and feed your little one, or let them practice guiding this to their mouth on their own. You can also simply let them use their hands and get a little messy and scoop up fistfuls.

Store in an airtight glass container in the fridge for up to 4 days or freezer for up to 3 months.

Food for Thought: The transition from a milk-only diet to incorporating solid foods can lead to constipation in some babies. To minimize discomfort, keep your baby hydrated (breast milk and small sips of water) along with plenty of fiber-rich foods. For my go-to constipation relief, see my Prune Puree on page 152.

Peaches & Cream

Yield: ½ cup (120 ml)

Who doesn't love this classic combination? We were lucky enough to be starting solids in the heart of the summer when Pepper was 6 months old. We live in "peach country" and have access to some amazing local peaches. To this day, I make this puree to add to my own cup of yogurt or morning bowl of oatmeal. Peaches are not only full of important vitamins and minerals, but they have been proven to help aid in digestion, which is something really important for your little one.

1 tbsp (15 ml) coconut oil

1 large peach, peeled, pitted and chopped

¼ tsp ground cinnamon

2 tbsp (30 ml) full-fat coconut cream (see Note)

Warm the coconut oil in a saucepan over medium heat. Add the peaches and cook, stirring occasionally, until the peaches soften, 5 to 8 minutes.

Remove the pan from the heat and add the contents to a high-speed blender or food processor along with the cinnamon and coconut cream.

For your beginner eater, serve about 1 tablespoon (15 ml) on a spoon and feed your little one, or let them practice guiding this to their mouth on their own. You can also simply let them use their hands and get a little messy and scoop up fistfuls.

Store in an airtight glass container in the fridge for up to 4 days or freezer for up to 3 months.

Variations: Try this with another stone fruit such as mangoes or apricots.

> **Note:** To avoid serving young babies foods that come from a can (even BPA-free cans contain harmful chemicals), I like to make coconut cream by blending equal parts coconut butter (which you can purchase in a glass jar) with hot water in a blender. Store in the fridge for up to 7 days.

Banana with Cardamom & Avocado

Yield: ½ cup (120 ml)

This is a wonderful little puree that is chock full of healthy fats and fiber and tastes amazing as well! Honestly, I make this often when I'm craving something sweet but need something healthy. Getting your little one used to interesting flavors (like cardamom) will hopefully pay off. I loved eating this puree right alongside my girls when they were first starting solids.

½ of a ripe avocado

½ of a ripe banana

1 tbsp (15 ml) plain whole-milk yogurt (goat, sheep or cow)

Pinch of cardamom

Place all the ingredients into a bowl and gently mash with the back of a fork.

For your beginner eater, serve about 1 tablespoon (15 ml) on a spoon and feed your little one, or let them practice guiding this to their mouth on their own. You can also simply let them use their hands and get a little messy and scoop up fistfuls.

This combination is best eaten the day you make it, as the avocado and banana brown up after a day in the fridge.

Beef & Carrot

Yield: ¾ cup (180 ml)

This was my go-to puree for Pepper when she first started solids. Iron-rich beef is an incredibly nutritious food with some of the most easily digestible vitamins and minerals for little bellies. Even the federal government has gotten on board with the importance of beef for young, growing children and, for the first time ever, has recommended feeding babies beef starting at 6 months old. It's rich in iron, zinc, vitamin B12, vitamin B6, selenium, riboflavin, phosphorus and choline, as well as plenty of protein. And you don't need to go crazy and spend a lot of money on a fancy cut of beef—1 pound (454 g) of grass-fed ground beef is the most economical.

¼ lb (113 g) ground beef

1 medium–small carrot, finely chopped

½ cup (120 ml) bone broth or water + more if needed

Place the beef and carrot in a saucepan and add the bone broth or water. Cover the pan and bring to a simmer. Cook until the beef is cooked through and the carrot is tender, about 8 minutes. Remove the pan from the heat and pour the contents into a food processor or high-speed blender. Process until smooth, adding more water or broth if needed to thin.

For your beginner eater, serve about 1 tablespoon (15 ml) on a spoon and feed your little one, or let them practice guiding this to their mouth on their own. You can also simply let them use their hands and get a little messy and scoop up fistfuls.

Store in an airtight glass container in the fridge for up to 3 days or freeze for up to 3 months.

Chicken Liver Pâté

Yield: 1 cup (240 ml)

Not only is liver one of the most economical foods to purchase, but it's one of the most nutrient-dense foods in the world. It contains all of the amino acids, which are the building blocks of protein that our bodies need to thrive. Babies and young children tend to be deficient in many of the vitamins and minerals found in liver, which is why this is a wonderful first food to serve. Keep in mind that it's naturally high in vitamin A. Vitamin A is a crucial nutrient but can become toxic if it's eaten in excess. For this reason, I'd recommend 1 tablespoon of paté twice a week for optimal nutrition without overdoing it. Making this pâté was a true joy for me, as I enjoyed spreading this on my sourdough toast with a fat pinch of flakey sea salt, while Pepper took hers straight up.

½ lb (226 g) chicken livers

1 cup (240 ml) whole milk

1 tbsp (14 g) unsalted butter or ghee

½ of a medium-sized apple, peeled, cored and chopped

½ of a yellow or red onion, finely chopped

Pinch of dried thyme

½ cup (120 ml) chicken bone broth or water + more if needed

Drain the chicken livers and coarsely chop them. Add them to a bowl with the milk. Let them soak in the milk from 1 to 3 hours in the fridge (this helps to minimize the strong flavor). Drain the livers and pat them dry.

Melt the butter or ghee in a saucepan over medium heat then add the apple, onion and thyme. Cook for about 7 minutes, or until softened. Add the liver and broth and bring to a low boil. Reduce the heat to medium-low and simmer until the liver is cooked through, 12 to 15 minutes.

Add the cooked mixture to the bowl of a food processor and process until smooth. If the mixture is too thick, add a touch more broth or water.

For your beginner eater, serve about 1 tablespoon (15 ml) on a spoon and feed your little one, or let them practice guiding this to their mouth on their own. You can also simply let them use their hands and get a little messy and scoop up fistfuls.

Pack the pâté in an airtight glass container and refrigerate for 5 days. If you want to extend the shelf life, pour a little melted butter, ghee or lard over the pâté. You can also freeze for up to 3 months.

Egg Yolk & Yogurt

Yield: ¼ cup (60 ml)

This is an easy and nutritious way to get some good fat, cholesterol, iron and probiotics into your little one. Eggs are a wonderful first food for your baby, as they contain many beneficial vitamins and minerals. However, the yolk is more easily digestible as a first food, so we have left the white out for this recipe. Once your baby tolerates the yolk, you can introduce the whole egg! If your baby has an egg allergy early on, rest assured most babies outgrow it and you can try again later (under the guidance of your pediatrician).

1 hard-boiled egg yolk

Pinch of dried thyme (optional)

2 tbsp (30 ml) plain whole-milk yogurt (sheep, goat or cow) + more if needed

Use the back of a fork to mash all the ingredients together. Add more yogurt to smooth this out as needed.

For your beginner eater, serve about 1 tablespoon (15 ml) on a spoon and feed your little one, or let them practice guiding this to their mouth on their own. You can also simply let them use their hands and get a little messy and scoop up fistfuls.

Store in an airtight glass container in the fridge for up to 3 days.

Part II:

Getting the Hang of Solids
(8 Months & Beyond)

Between 8 and 13 months, Pepper's curiosity and willingness to try new things was a given—and something I totally took for granted in retrospect! I had no idea what was lurking around the corner (Hint: a very opinionated and stubborn eater!), so if you are just entering this delightful stage of "yes!" and "more!" I really hope you enjoy it.

During this period of development, most babies really do eat almost anything you put in front of them (of course there are exceptions). Turns out, when I asked our pediatrician about this, it seems that a lot of babies haven't formed strong opinions about food yet and are eager to explore their plates, so it's a great time to continue introducing interesting flavors and textures to build that strong and robust foundation.

I also found that, as we were introducing more textured foods, it was helpful to research how to cut and serve the food I was preparing for her. The website Solid Starts (solidstarts.com) has a great guide on how to chop or slice pieces of whole foods for your little eater.

One thing I learned was that smaller, diced-up pieces were easier for young babies to swallow whole, which made them a potential choking hazard. But if a baby was holding and gumming part of a larger piece of food—like one of my Salmon Nuggets (page 63)— they would naturally work to break it down into something easier to swallow.

I have no affiliation with the Solid Starts website, but if you are in this stage of feeding your baby, I really do recommend checking it out. It was such a useful resource for me because it allows you to search for suggestions on how to chop or serve a particular food to a child of a certain age. (For example, smash blueberries and raspberries between your fingers to make them less of a choking hazard for young children.)

> **Food for Thought:** Sometimes if Pepper wasn't trying a new food, I would serve it alongside a food I knew she loved. We referred to this as her "safe" food. For us, that was usually sliced avocado or plain yogurt. Eating begets eating and oftentimes after she would eat her avocado she would then reach for the salmon nugget or meatball.

In the recipes that follow, I also give a few suggestions on serving the actual food (i.e., slice, mash, put on a spoon or serve whole). As always, watch your baby closely and try to stay relaxed and enjoy the process. The recipes that follow (while designed for your new eater) are also recipes that I hope you will enjoy for years to come (even long after your kids are out of the house). In all honesty, I can't believe I lived almost 39 years without experiencing the joys of a salmon nugget or a savory breakfast muffin!

> **Food for Thought:** You will notice that salt is an option to use sparingly in the recipes that follow. Most conventional pediatric advice on foods before the age of 1 are to avoid all foods containing salt. Through my own research and talking with naturopathic pediatricians, I've learned that a pinch of unrefined salt can help with digestion and supplies a variety of trace minerals. Used sparingly, it can be part of a healthy diet for a baby. Of course, skip salt if it doesn't feel right to you.

ABC Muffins (Apple, Beet, Carrot)

Yield: 24 mini muffins

These are a Bemis family favorite. We love making these all summer and fall when the carrots and beets are cranking at the farm. These muffins make a wonderful on-the-go snack and are loaded with nourishing ingredients for your little one. Buckwheat is a gluten-free grain and has a more complex and nuttier flavor than whole-wheat flour. I liked introducing this grain when Pepper was younger because I wanted her to get used to stronger flavors in baked goods. The grains are soaked overnight in yogurt, which helps to make them easier to digest and more nutritious.

½ cup (60 g) buckwheat flour

½ cup (60 g) millet flour (see Note)

½ cup (120 ml) plain whole-milk yogurt (goat, sheep or cow)

½ tsp baking soda

½ tsp ground cinnamon

½ tsp ground ginger

¼ tsp ground nutmeg

1 egg, beaten

½ cup (120 ml) unsweetened applesauce

3 tbsp (45 ml) melted coconut oil

½ cup (55 g) shredded carrots

½ cup (55 g) shredded beets

The evening before baking, whisk together the flours and yogurt in a large bowl. Cover with a dish towel and place in a warm spot in your kitchen overnight. If using sprouted grains, you can skip this part.

The next morning, preheat the oven to 350°F (175°C). Line a mini-muffin tin with parchment paper liners or lightly grease the tin. Set it aside.

Add the baking soda, cinnamon, ginger and nutmeg to the bowl with the flour mixture. Use a wooden spatula to mix it in (the dough will feel gummy at first and that's totally normal!). Add the beaten egg, applesauce and melted coconut oil. Mix to combine. Fold in the shredded veggies and fill each muffin cup with 3 tablespoons (45 ml) of the batter. Bake in the oven for 18 to 20 minutes or until golden brown and a toothpick inserted in the center of a muffin comes out clean.

Serve to your baby whole and let them grip/mash the muffins and guide them to their mouth, or crumble a muffin and serve to your baby on a spoon with yogurt.

Store in a sealed glass or stainless-steel container in the fridge for up to 4 days or freeze for up to 3 months. Gently reheat in the oven or a toaster oven for a few minutes before serving (optional). These taste great as is or drizzled with nut butter and additional cinnamon.

Note: Grains can be tricky to digest for young babies. It's important to purchase sprouted grains or to soak your grains overnight before cooking them.

2-Ingredient Pancakes 3 Ways

These pancakes saved me during the transition from purees to more textured foods. Not only are they a breeze to whip up, but they're loaded with protein and veggies. Eggs are essential for brain development, and the vitamins and minerals from the eggs and veggies combined make these little cakes a powerhouse of a "meal" for new eaters. These pancakes are delicious and taste great drizzled with nut butter, yogurt or a dollop of butter. I eat these right along with my daughter when I make them and they're always a hit. The batter is way more delicate than traditional pancake batter and it may take a few pancakes to get the hang of it. A few tips: Make these pancakes small. Think silver dollar–sized pancakes. That makes them cook more evenly and easier to flip. Also, keep the pan well greased with a healthy fat (ghee, butter, tallow or coconut oil) and keep the temperature to medium-low. A thin, metal spatula is perfect for flipping.

Beet Pancakes

Yield: 8 silver dollar–sized pancakes

Heaping ½ cup (140 ml) pureed cooked beets (from about 1 large beet)

2 eggs

¼ tsp dried thyme (optional)

2–3 tbsp (30–45 ml) ghee or coconut oil

Plain yogurt or nut butter for topping (optional)

Whisk together the pureed beets and eggs. Add the optional seasonings of your choice.

Heat the ghee or coconut oil (or your favorite cooking fat) in a large cast-iron skillet over medium-low heat. When the oil is warm, drop the batter by the heaping tablespoon (15 ml; think silver dollar–sized) and cook undisturbed for 3 to 5 minutes.

Use a thin metal spatula to carefully lift a tiny corner of the pancake to make sure it is browned nicely. Gently flip the pancakes and cook for an additional 2 to 3 minutes.

Serve the pancakes to your little one as is, or slice into thin strips. Feel free to drizzle with nut butter, yogurt or a dollop of unsalted grass-fed butter.

Store in an airtight glass container in the fridge for up to 3 days.

Sweet Potato Spiced Pancakes

Yield: 6 silver dollar–sized pancakes

Heaping ½ cup (140 ml) mashed cooked sweet potato (avoid canned sweet potatoes as they contain too much liquid)

2 eggs

½ tsp ground cinnamon (optional)

¼ tsp ground ginger (optional)

⅛ tsp ground nutmeg (optional)

2–3 tbsp (30–45 ml) ghee or coconut oil

Plain yogurt or nut butter for topping (optional)

Whisk together the sweet potato and eggs. Add optional seasonings.

Heat the ghee or coconut oil (or your favorite cooking fat) in a large cast-iron skillet over medium-low heat (you want to avoid a very hot pan, or these will burn without cooking through). When the oil is warm, drop the batter by the heaping tablespoon (15ml; think silver dollar–sized) and cook undisturbed for 3 to 4 minutes. Use a thin metal spatula to carefully lift a tiny corner of the pancake to make sure it is browned nicely. Gently flip the pancakes and cook for an additional 2 to 3 minutes.

Serve the pancakes to your little one as is, or slice into thin strips. Feel free to drizzle with nut butter, yogurt or a dollop of butter.

Store in an airtight glass container in the fridge for up to 3 days.

Banana Spinach Pancakes

Yield: 6 silver dollar–sized pancakes

Heaping ½ cup (160 g) mashed banana (from about 1 large banana)

Small handful baby spinach, roughly chopped

2 eggs

½ tsp ground cardamom (optional)

2–3 tbsp (30–45 ml) ghee or coconut oil

Plain yogurt or nut butter for topping (optional)

Whisk together the mashed banana, spinach and eggs. Add the cardamom, if using.

Heat the ghee or coconut oil (or your favorite cooking fat) in a large cast-iron skillet over medium-low heat. When the oil is warm, drop the batter by the heaping tablespoon (15 ml; think silver dollar–sized) and cook undisturbed for 3 to 5 minutes. Use a thin metal spatula to carefully lift a tiny corner of the pancake to make sure it is browned nicely. Gently flip the pancakes and cook for an additional 2 to 3 minutes.

Serve the pancakes to your little one as is, or slice into thin strips. Feel free to drizzle with nut butter, yogurt or a dollop of butter.

Store in an airtight glass container in the fridge for up to 3 days.

Curried Red Lentil & Pumpkin Falafel

Yield: 20 patties

These are a wonderful transitional food for a new eater. They are soft to chew, packed with a ton of nutrition, and full of bold flavors to get your little one used to spice. I like to serve these with a little tahini, but plain whole-milk yogurt would be equally delicious. This is a recipe the whole family can enjoy together. A side of rice and roasted veggies can make this a lovely complete meal for older children and adults.

1 cup (192 g) dried red lentils, soaked in water for at least 8 hours or overnight

½ cup (123 g) roasted mashed pumpkin (or any variety of winter squash)

½ cup (46 g) chickpea flour (sprouted if possible; see Note on page 41)

2 cloves garlic, peeled and chopped

1 tsp smoked paprika

1 tsp ground cumin

1 tsp ground coriander

½ tsp ground cinnamon

¼ tsp unrefined salt (optional if serving to a baby under 1)

Drizzle of well-stirred tahini or plain whole-milk yogurt, for serving

Preheat the oven to 350°F (175°C). Liberally grease a baking sheet with ghee, butter, coconut oil or another nourishing fat and set it aside.

Drain the soaked lentils and give them a good rinse. Bring a large pot of water to a boil, add the lentils, and cook for 8 minutes (you are only partially cooking these). Drain.

Add the drained lentils, pumpkin, chickpea flour, garlic, paprika, cumin, coriander, cinnamon and salt (if using) to a food processor. Pulse the mixture ten to fifteen times or until it just comes together but still has some texture. Use your hands to scoop out about 1½-tablespoon (25-g)-sized portions of the batter and roll between your palms. The batter will be wet and that is okay! If it's too wet for you to form patties, place the batter in the fridge for 25 minutes to firm up a bit. Place each ball on the prepared baking sheet and use your palm or the back of a spoon to lightly flatten the mixture into a "patty." Repeat with the remaining batter.

Bake in the oven until lightly golden brown, 15 to 18 minutes. Be careful to not overbake these or the mixture will become dry, which is tough for beginner eaters to handle. Drizzle with tahini or plain whole-milk yogurt.

To serve, slice into thin strips and let your little one practice their pincer grasp or lightly mash and place on a spoon.

Store in an airtight glass container in the fridge for up to 3 days.

Savory Veggie Muffins

Yield: 24 mini muffins

These veggie muffins are hands down one of my favorite on-the-go snacks for a new eater or busy toddler. They're loaded with nourishing ingredients like broccoli, sweet potatoes, protein-packed yogurt and hearty buckwheat flour. I hope you and your little ones love these muffins as much as we do.

½ cup (60 g) buckwheat flour

½ cup (60 g) millet flour (see Note)

¾ cup (180 ml) plain whole-milk yogurt

½ tsp baking soda

½ tsp garlic powder

½ tsp onion powder

¼ tsp paprika

½ tsp fine sea salt (optional if serving to a baby under 1)

2 tbsp (10 g) nutritional yeast (optional)

1 egg, beaten

¼ cup (60 ml) melted unsalted butter, ghee or olive oil

½ cup (54 g) shredded Swiss cheese

½ cup (64 g) shredded sweet potato

½ cup (50 g) finely chopped/ minced broccoli florets (this works well in a food processor)

The evening before baking, whisk together the flours and yogurt in a large bowl. Cover with a dish towel and place in a warm spot in your kitchen overnight.

The next morning, preheat the oven to 350°F (175°C).

Line a mini-muffin tin with parchment paper liners or lightly grease the tin. Set it aside.

Add the baking soda, garlic powder, onion powder, paprika and salt and nutritional yeast (if using) to the bowl of dough. Use a wooden spatula to mix (the dough will feel gummy at first and that's totally normal). Add the beaten egg and melted butter. Mix to combine. Fold in the cheese and veggies and divide the batter between the muffin cups.

Bake for 18 to 20 minutes or until golden brown and a toothpick inserted in the center of a muffin comes out clean.

Serve to your baby whole and let them grip/mash the muffins and guide them to their mouth, or crumble a muffin and serve on a spoon with yogurt.

Store in a sealed glass container in the fridge for up to 4 days or freeze for up to 3 months. Gently reheat in the oven or a toaster oven for a few minutes before serving (optional). These taste great with a little dollop of unsalted grass-fed butter for serving.

Note: I love millet flour and find it a great grain to have in my pantry for baking and cooking. However, if you can't find millet flour (I order mine from Second Spring Foods) you can substitute all-purpose flour.

Eggs 4 Ways

The humble egg is nature's perfect food and an important first food for your little one. I mentioned in the Egg Yolk & Yogurt recipe (page 35) that introducing egg yolks first is important, as the yolks are easier to digest than the whites. If your baby tolerates the yolks just fine, then you are ready to introduce the whole egg. Eggs contain more than 6 grams of high-quality protein and at least fourteen essential vitamins and minerals that are important for brain development and growth. Because eggs can be a common allergen for babies, it's recommended to introduce them early and often. Studies have shown that early and repeated exposure in infancy can help prevent an egg allergy from developing. And if your baby does develop an egg allergy, rest assured that more than 70 percent of babies outgrow the allergy.

I think eggs are magic because not only are they nourishing, but you can prepare them in so many ways. I am sharing four of my go-to methods, and I hope you enjoy these easy, no-fuss eggs for you and your little ones.

Curry Pumpkin Soft Scrambled Eggs

Yield: 1 adult and 1 baby serving

1 tbsp (15 ml) coconut oil

2 eggs

1 tbsp (15 ml) water

2 heaping tbsp (35 ml) roasted pumpkin puree (or any winter squash)

¼ tsp mild curry powder

Pinch of salt (optional if serving to a baby under 1)

Melt the coconut oil in a small cast-iron skillet over medium-low heat.

In a bowl, whisk the eggs, water, pumpkin, curry powder and salt (if using).

Add the egg mixture to the skillet and watch for the edges to just barely set, then use a rubber spatula to gently swipe around the edges of the pan to create large, soft curds. Do not flip the curds over, just continue to gently swipe and fold the liquid eggs until the entire pan has formed large soft curds of lightly set eggs. Once the eggs are set, remove the pan from the heat.

Wait until the eggs have cooled enough before serving them to your little one. Serve to your baby on a spoon or fork, or let them use their hands to grab small handfuls and guide the food to their mouth on their own.

For moms and dads enjoying these eggs with your babe, I recommend a slice of sourdough toast to accompany your soft scramble.

Store in an airtight glass container in the fridge for up to 3 days.

Baby's First Egg Salad

Yield: ½ cup (110 g)

2 hard-boiled eggs, peeled

2 tbsp (30 ml) plain whole-milk yogurt

2 tsp (10 ml) sauerkraut juice (optional)

Pinch of dried thyme

Mash the eggs in a bowl and stir in the yogurt, sauerkraut juice and thyme.

Serve your baby on a spoon or let them use their hands to guide small handfuls straight into their mouth.

Store leftovers in the fridge for up to 3 days.

Simple Hard-Boiled Eggs

Yield: 2 eggs

2 eggs

Pinch of chili powder or paprika (optional)

Bring a pot of water to a boil.

Add the eggs, lower the heat to a low boil and cook for about 10 minutes.

Remove the pot from the heat and rinse the eggs under cold water.

When cool, peel the eggs, then slice them in half or in quarters and sprinkle with chili powder or paprika (if using). Let your baby grab each piece and gnaw on it. Or use a spoon to mash the egg and let your baby spoon feed themselves.

Store in an airtight glass container in the fridge for up to 3 days.

Mini Sweet Potato Frittata

Yield: One 6-inch (15-cm) frittata

3 eggs

1½ tbsp (23 ml) water

¼ cup (60 g) cooked and mashed sweet potato

½ tsp smoked paprika

½ tsp garlic powder

½ tsp onion powder

Pinch of salt (optional if serving to a baby under 1)

1–2 tbsp (15–30 ml) ghee or butter

Preheat the oven to 375°F (190°C).

In a large bowl, combine the eggs, water, sweet potato, paprika, garlic powder, onion powder and salt (if using) and whisk until evenly incorporated.

Melt the ghee or butter in a mini cast-iron skillet over medium heat. Add the egg mixture to the pan and let it just barely set. Use a rubber spatula to gently lift the just-set eggs and let the uncooked eggs run beneath. Repeat this process for about 2 minutes.

Remove the pan from the heat and place it in the oven. Bake until the frittata has set, 10 to 12 minutes (checking around the 9-minute mark).

Once cool enough to handle, slice the frittata into long thin strips. Let your baby grab a strip to gnaw on, or you can crumble the frittata and serve over plain whole-milk yogurt.

Store in an airtight glass container in the fridge for up to 3 days.

Note: Long strips are easier for your baby to grasp and hold. Let them gnaw and bite into each strip and practice their pincer grasp.

Pumpkin Meatballs

Yield: 20 meatballs

I absolutely love these meatballs!! They are super moist (thanks to the roasted pumpkin), which makes them easier for a young baby to eat. These meatballs are spiced with fall flavors like cinnamon and sage and are also repurposed later in the book under the Family Dinners section in my Autumn Spiced Spaghetti and Meatballs recipe (page 119). Another reason I love these so much is simply because they're made with red meat. Red meat is one of the most nutritious whole foods around and is a key source of iron. Iron does not get passed through breast milk and a lot of babies tend to be low in this mineral. Having these meatballs on regular rotation is a great way to keep iron levels up while also enjoying a tasty meal. These work well with any ground red meat such as beef, lamb, bison or wild game.

1 lb (454 g) ground beef

½ cup (123 g) roasted pumpkin, mashed

1½ tsp (1 g) dried sage

1 tsp ground cinnamon

¼ tsp ground nutmeg

¼ tsp garlic powder

¼ tsp unrefined salt (optional if serving to a baby under 1)

1 egg, whisked

Preheat the oven to 350°F (175°C). Lightly grease a baking sheet.

In a large bowl, mix the beef, pumpkin, sage, cinnamon, nutmeg, garlic powder, salt (if using) and egg. Place the mixture in the fridge for 30 minutes to chill (this will make forming the meatballs easier, as it is a wet batter).

When chilled, remove the mixture from the fridge and use your hands to form the meat into 1-inch (2.5-cm) meatballs.

Place on the greased baking sheet and bake until cooked through, about 20 minutes.

Serve the meatballs with Tomato–Sage Sauce (page 119) or simply as is. For a young baby, you can serve the meatballs whole and let them gnaw on them. Or slice the meatballs into long finger-width slices and let them practice their pincer grasp and feed themselves. You can also mash a meatball and serve it to your babe on a spoon.

Store in an airtight glass container in the fridge for up to 3 days.

Carrot Fries

Yield: 4 servings

These are delicious, and we have totally moved on from regular potato fries on burger night and opt for carrot fries instead! Carrots are full of antioxidants and are a great source of vitamin K. We toss these fries in melted ghee, which not only adds more nutrients to the fries but also has a wonderful, buttery flavor. These fries are perfectly spiced and taste great dipped into homemade Date-Sweetened Ketchup (page 85) or Greek Yogurt Ranch (page 84). These fries are wonderful for the whole family, and I hope you and your little ones enjoy them as much as we do.

1½ lb (680 g) carrots, about 6–8 medium, peeled and cut into matchsticks

2 tbsp (30 ml) melted ghee or duck fat

½ tsp garlic powder

½ tsp onion powder

¼ tsp smoked paprika

¼ tsp dried thyme or rosemary

½ tsp unrefined salt (optional if serving to a baby under 1)

Preheat the oven to 425°F (220°C) and place an oven rack in the upper third of the oven. Grease two baking sheets with ghee or another cooking fat and set aside.

In a large bowl, toss the carrots with the melted ghee, garlic powder, onion powder, paprika, thyme and salt (if using). Scatter the carrots between the two baking sheets, being careful to not overcrowd the pans. Bake for 30 to 40 minutes or until tender and golden brown, flipping halfway through the cook time.

Serve as is, or mash the carrots and place them on a spoon with a little yogurt and let your baby guide the spoon to their mouth.

These fries are best enjoyed the same day they are made.

Veggie Cheese Balls 3 Ways

These veggie cheese balls are delicious! They are a great transitional food for new eaters, and you can expose your little ones to bold flavors with the addition of spices and herbs.

I started serving these to Pepper when she was around 9 months and would just let her gnaw away at a whole ball. Remember, your baby may be ready for these closer to 7 or 8 months. They'll let you know! If you're making these for older toddlers, try adding a dip when you serve them. Now that Pepper is two, she loves dipping her veggie balls into homemade Date-Sweetened Ketchup (page 85) or Greek Yogurt Ranch (page 84). Also, if you are serving these to an older toddler, you can use a stronger tasting cheese like sharp Cheddar (which is good to avoid with young babies, as it's higher in sodium)—it will add a little more flavor. These days we love making the Carrot Swiss Bites and Zucchini Herb Bites with Cheddar instead, for a different twist! These three recipes taste delicious slightly warm, but can easily be sent in a school lunch box and eaten cold or at room temperature.

Carrot Swiss Bites

Yield: 12 bites

1½ cups (165 g) grated carrots

½ cup (54 g) grated Swiss cheese (try extra-sharp Cheddar for older toddlers)

⅓ cup (32 g) almond flour (or finely ground sourdough bread-crumbs)

1 egg, beaten

½ tsp smoked paprika

¼ tsp garlic powder

¼ tsp onion powder

¼ tsp unrefined salt (optional if making for a baby under 1)

Preheat the oven to 400°F (205°C). Liberally grease a baking sheet or line it with parchment paper and set it aside.

Squeeze as much moisture out of the carrots as possible using a dish towel. (Save the juice for sipping or adding to a smoothie!) If you're serving these to a very young eater, you have the option to mince up the grated carrots even smaller. For more advanced babies, there is no need to do that.

Add the carrots to a large bowl and mix in the Swiss cheese, almond flour, egg, paprika, garlic powder, onion powder and salt (if using). Scoop out tablespoon-sized (15-g) portions and roll into balls between your palms. The mixture will be wet; that's normal and totally okay! These don't have to be perfectly shaped.

Place on the well-greased or parchment paper–lined baking sheet and bake in the oven until golden brown, 15 to 18 minutes.

To serve, either give a whole ball to your little one and let them gnaw on it, or slice the balls in half. You can also crumble a ball and serve over plain whole milk yogurt.

Store in a glass airtight container in the fridge for up to 4 days or freeze for up to 3 months.

Zucchini Herb Bites

Yield: 12 bites

1½ cups (186 g) shredded zucchini

½ cup (56 g) grated mozzarella cheese (try extra-sharp Cheddar for older toddlers)

⅓ cup (32 g) almond flour or finely ground sourdough bread-crumbs

1 egg, beaten

¼ tsp onion powder

¼ tsp garlic powder

½ tsp dried dill

½ tsp dried parsley

¼ tsp unrefined salt (optional if you're making for a baby under 1)

Preheat the oven to 400°F (205°C). Liberally grease or line a baking sheet with parchment paper and set it aside.

Squeeze as much moisture out of the zucchini as possible using a dish towel. You really want to get as much moisture out as possible. (Save the juice for sipping or adding to a smoothie!) If you are serving these to a very young eater, you have the option to mince up the grated zucchini even more. For more advanced babies, there is no need to do that.

Add the zucchini to a large bowl and mix in the mozzarella, almond flour, egg, onion powder, garlic powder, dill, parsley and salt (if using). Scoop out tablespoon-sized (15-g) portions and roll into balls between your palms. The mixture will be wet; that's okay! These don't have to be perfectly shaped.

Place on the well-greased or parchment paper–lined baking sheet and bake in the oven until golden brown, 15 to 18 minutes.

To serve, either give a whole ball to your little one and let them gnaw on it, or slice the balls in half. You can also crumble a ball and serve it over plain whole-milk yogurt.

Store in a glass airtight container in the fridge for up to 4 days or freeze for up to 3 months.

Cheesy Cauliflower Curry Bites

Yield: 12 bites

2 cups (200 g) cauliflower florets

½ cup (56 g) grated mozzarella cheese

⅓ cup (32 g) almond flour or finely ground sourdough bread-crumbs

1 egg, whisked

½ tsp mild curry powder

¼ tsp garlic powder

¼ tsp onion powder

¼ tsp unrefined salt (optional if you're feeding these to a baby under 1)

Preheat the oven to 400°F (205°C). Liberally grease a baking sheet and set it aside.

Place the cauliflower florets in a food processor and pulse until the cauliflower has the consistency of rice. Remove the cauliflower from the processor. (You should have about 1½ cups [170 g] of "riced" cauliflower.) Place the cauliflower in a dish towel and squeeze out as much moisture as possible.

Place the cauliflower in a large bowl along with the mozzarella, almond flour, egg, curry powder, garlic powder, onion powder and salt (if using) and mix well. Form the mixture into tablespoon-sized (15 g) balls between your palms. The mixture will be wet; that's normal and totally okay! These don't have to be perfectly shaped.

Place on the prepared baking sheet. Bake in the oven until lightly browned and crisp, 15 to 18 minutes.

To serve, either give a whole ball to your little one and let them gnaw on it, or slice the balls in half. You can also crumble a ball and serve it over plain whole-milk yogurt.

Store leftovers in an airtight glass container in the fridge for up to 4 days or freeze for up to 3 months.

Food for Thought: One of the most liberating mindset shifts I've made when it comes to feeding my children is this: I get to choose the food that goes on their plate. They get to choose what does or doesn't go into their mouth. Rest assured as you continue to model eating the foods that you want your children to eat, they'll most likely begin to follow suit. As always, there are exceptions to this, and reach out to your pediatrician if you are concerned about eating habits.

Salmon Nuggets

Yield: 12 small nuggets

These little salmon nuggets are delicious, portable and a winner for your beginner eater and for the whole family. Salmon is a wonderful first food for your young eater because it contains many essential nutrients that babies need to thrive. Packed with vitamin D, iron, zinc and omega-3 fatty acids (which are essential for brain development), these little nuggets are a wonderful recipe to keep on rotation. If I'm making these for adults, too, I sometimes panfry the baked nuggets after they're cooked to get a crispy crust. But honestly, they taste awesome fresh out of the oven, too.

We love these dipped in plain yogurt or homemade Date-Sweetened Ketchup (page 85). These also freeze well, so feel free to double the recipe, especially if you're making them for the whole family. To make this part of a complete family meal, I suggest serving with a side of Deviled Cauliflower Mash (page 22) and a simple salad.

½ lb (226 g) salmon filet

A little melted ghee or olive oil for drizzling on the salmon

¼ cup (60 ml) plain whole-milk yogurt

1 egg, lightly beaten

¼ cup (25 g) almond flour or finely ground sourdough breadcrumbs

½ tsp garlic powder

½ tsp onion powder

½ tsp dried dill

¼ tsp unrefined salt (optional if you're feeding these to a baby under 1)

Preheat the oven to 400°F (205°C) and liberally grease a baking sheet.

Place the salmon on the greased baking sheet and drizzle with a little melted ghee or olive oil. Bake in the oven until barely cooked through, 12 to 14 minutes, being careful to not overcook the salmon. (You will bake it again after you form the nuggets.)

Remove the salmon from the oven and, when it is cool enough to handle, use a fork to flake the fish and remove any bones. Add the flaked salmon to the bowl of a food processor and pulse until well mashed. Add the yogurt, egg, almond flour, garlic powder, onion powder, dill and salt (if using) and pulse a few more times or until all the ingredients are well incorporated.

Place the mixture in the fridge for about 20 minutes to firm up a bit.

(continued)

Salmon Nuggets

(continued)

After chilling, remove the salmon from the fridge and use your hands to form the mixture into tablespoon-sized (15-g) "nuggets" and place on the prepared baking sheet. The mixture will be wet, and that's okay. These don't have to be perfectly shaped. Bake in the oven until lightly browned, 15 to 18 minutes.

For a young baby, you can serve the nuggets whole and let them gnaw on them. You can also mash a nugget and serve it to your babe on a spoon with some yogurt. For older toddlers, let them dip the nuggets into their favorite condiment.

Store in an airtight glass container in the fridge for up to 4 days. Leftovers can be enjoyed cold, or reheated in a 350°F (175°C) oven for 10 to 12 minutes.

Food for Thought: The magic of three! I learned from the website Solid Starts that when your baby is a bit older (around 1) try serving each "meal" with three different foods on their plate. Sometimes if you just offer a plate of scrambled eggs your baby will be turned off by only one option and not touch a thing. However, if you put a small portion of scrambled eggs with two other foods, they may be more inclined to try a bite of all three things! This was a game changer for us when Pepper one day decided (full stop!) that she hated scrambled eggs. Turns out, she still loved them, she just liked them better when they were served alongside a tiny portion of avocado and cheese.

Pumpkin Banana Buckwheat Muffins

Yield: 24 mini muffins

These are a delicious morning treat the whole family will love. They are naturally sweetened with roasted winter squash and mashed banana. The warming spices of cinnamon, nutmeg and cloves make them seem sweeter than they really are. With that being said, if you are accustomed to sweeter baked goods, it will take a short time for your taste buds to adjust to less sweet treats. For a baby who hasn't had any added sugars in their diet yet, they'll never know the difference! As in the ABC Muffins (page 41), the grains are soaked overnight to aid digestion and increase nutrition.

½ cup (60 g) buckwheat flour

½ cup (60 g) millet flour

¾ cup (180 ml) plain whole-milk yogurt

½ tsp baking soda

½ tsp unrefined salt (optional if making for a baby under 1)

1 tsp ground cinnamon

¼ tsp ground nutmeg

1 egg, beaten

½ tsp vanilla extract

3 tbsp (45 ml) melted butter, ghee or coconut oil

1 overripe banana, mashed (about ½ cup [150 g])

½ cup (123 g) roasted mashed winter squash (pumpkin, Hubbard, delicata, butternut, etc.)

The evening before baking, mix the buckwheat and millet flours with the yogurt in a large bowl and place in a warm spot in your kitchen. Cover with a dish towel.

The following morning, preheat the oven to 350°F (175°C). Line a 24-cup mini-muffin tin with parchment liners and set aside.

Add the baking soda, salt (if using), cinnamon, nutmeg, egg, vanilla, butter, banana and squash to the bowl with the flour mixture and stir. (The mixture will feel "gummy," which is totally normal, and the muffins will cook up just fine!)

Fill each muffin cup three quarters full, then bake in the oven until a toothpick comes out clean when inserted into the center of a muffin, 15 to 18 minutes.

Serve muffins slightly warmed with a drizzle of nut butter for good measure!

Store the muffins in the fridge for up to 4 days or freeze for up to 3 months. Leftovers can be enjoyed cold, or reheated in a 350°F (175°C) oven for 10 to 12 minutes.

Nourishing Beef & Millet Nuggets

Yield: 30 nuggets

These little nuggets are a powerhouse of a meal. They pack a ton of veggies into each bite, and the millet adds some extra fiber. Beef liver contains significant amounts of folate, iron, vitamin B, vitamin A and copper, and eating a single serving can help meet your daily recommendation of all these vitamins and minerals. Liver has a stronger flavor, so we soak it in milk for an hour before preparing the recipe to help mellow out the flavor a bit and, when it is mixed with the rest of the ingredients, it is basically hidden in these nuggets! With that being said, if you don't have beef liver on hand or can't get it at your local grocery store, you can omit the liver and these turn out just as well. These nuggets freeze well and are great for meal prep for school lunches. You can place a frozen nugget in a lunch box and it will be thawed by noon!

¼ lb (113 g) beef or chicken liver, roughly chopped

1 cup (240 ml) milk (for soaking)

1 lb (454 g) ground beef

1 cup (175 g) cooked millet (see Note)

2 large cloves garlic, roughly chopped

1 cup (128 g) roughly chopped carrots

½ cup (30 g) roughly chopped parsley

½ cup (80 g) roughly chopped onion

1 tsp dried oregano

½ tsp unrefined salt (optional if feeding to a baby under 1)

Drain the liver then place it in a bowl and cover it with the milk. Soak for 1 to 3 hours in the fridge. Drain the liver and pat dry. Pulse the liver in a food processor until minced. Add the liver to a large bowl and mix in the ground beef and millet. To the bowl of the same food processor add the garlic, chopped carrot, parsley and onion and process until finely chopped. Add to the bowl with the beef/millet mixture and stir. Season with oregano and salt (if using) and stir again.

Preheat the oven to 350°F (175°C) and lightly grease a baking sheet.

Form the mixture into little "nuggets" about 1 inch (2.5 cm) long and place on the prepared baking sheet. Bake in the oven until cooked through, 20 to 25 minutes depending on the size of your nuggets.

Serve to your baby whole, sliced into thin strips or crumbled onto whole-milk yogurt.

Store in an airtight glass container in the fridge for up to 4 days. Leftovers can be enjoyed cold, or reheated in a 350°F (175°C) oven for 10 to 12 minutes.

Note: For easier digestion, use millet that was soaked prior to cooking, or use sprouted millet.

Green Monster Muffins

Yield: 9 muffins

Don't worry, these "Green Monster" muffins are a friendly muffin. Pepper loves these, and I love how many nourishing ingredients I can pack into them! More than anything though, she really loves helping me dump everything into our blender and pressing the button! These muffins are absolutely delicious and so fun and easy to make with your little one because everything gets whipped up in a blender. They are naturally sweetened with fiber-rich dates and applesauce and are extremely moist.

½ cup (60 g) Medjool dates, pitted and chopped (about 5 large dates)

½ cup (120 ml) unsweetened applesauce

½ cup (120 ml) plain whole-milk yogurt (goat, sheep or cow)

¼ cup (65 g) nut butter (almond, peanut, hazelnut or cashew will all work well!)

1 egg

1 tsp vanilla extract

1½–2 cups (45–60 g) loosely packed spinach (if using large leaves roughly chop them)

1 cup (120 g) sprouted oat flour (see Note on page 41)

¼ tsp baking soda

1 tsp ground cinnamon

¼ tsp ground nutmeg

½ tsp unrefined salt (optional if serving to a baby under 1)

Preheat the oven to 350°F (175°C) and line a muffin tin with parchment liners (or generously grease the pan with butter, ghee or coconut oil).

Soak the dates in a bowl of boiling water for 10 minutes to soften them.

Add the soaked dates to a high-speed blender or food processor along with the applesauce, yogurt, nut butter, egg and vanilla extract. Blend on high until the mixture comes together and the dates are well incorporated. Add the spinach, oat flour, baking soda, cinnamon, nutmeg and salt (if using) and blend on high until well combined.

Spoon the mixture into the prepared muffin tin and bake in the oven until a toothpick inserted into the center of a muffin comes out clean, 20 to 25 minutes.

Serve the muffins to your baby whole, or slice muffins into thin strips. Spread with grass-fed butter or drizzle with additional nut butter if desired.

Store muffins in a glass or stainless-steel container in the fridge for up to 5 days. Gently reheat in the oven or let them come to room temperature before enjoying.

Cheesy Cauliflower Fritters

Yield: 12 small fritters

These little fritters are not only a fan favorite among little eaters, but older kids and adults love these just as much. We have made these dozens of times to share with friends and family, and everyone raves about them no matter what their age! We like to serve these with our Date-Sweetened Ketchup (page 85) or Greek Yogurt Ranch (page 84) for a fun appetizer for the whole family.

3 cups (340 g) finely chopped cauliflower (from about 1 small head)

¾ cup (84 g) mozzarella cheese (if serving to a baby over 1 you can use a stronger tasting cheese like sharp Cheddar)

½ cup (46 g) sprouted chickpea flour (see Note on page 41)

1 large egg, whisked

3 green onions, finely chopped (white and pale green parts)

2 cloves garlic, mined

Pinch of crushed red pepper flakes (optional)

½ tsp unrefined salt (optional if serving to a baby under 1)

Ghee, duck fat, tallow or coconut oil for frying

Bring a large pot of water to a boil and add the chopped cauliflower. Simmer for about 5 minutes. Drain and let the cauliflower sit until it is cool enough to handle.

To a large bowl, add the chopped cauliflower, along with the cheese, flour, egg, green onions, garlic, pepper flakes (if using) and salt (if using). Mash the mixture with a wooden spoon or fork.

Add the cooking fat to a large cast-iron skillet over medium-high heat. Use a ¼-cup (60-ml) measuring cup to scoop out small portions of the batter (don't fill the measuring cup all the way, as these are a bit fragile and smaller patties are easier to work with) and place the mixture into the hot skillet. Lightly press the batter down and fry each fritter for about 3 minutes per side or until lightly browned and crisp. A metal spatula works best for flipping. Remove from the pan and place on a paper towel–lined plate to drain excess cooking fat.

To serve, place a whole fritter on the high chair or tray and let your baby guide it to their mouth, or slice these into thin strips.

Store in an airtight glass container in the fridge for up to 3 days. Leftovers can be enjoyed cold, or reheated in a 300°F (150°C) oven for 10 to 12 minutes.

3-Ingredient Banana Oat Bites

Yield: 10 small cookies

These are a fun and tasty first cookie for your baby. They're great because they store well in your fridge (for at least a month), or you can freeze them for up to 3 months and thaw them before serving your little one. It's important to use sprouted oat flour for these, as oats are hard to digest and babies are the most vulnerable to having issues digesting them. The batter is definitely "wet" and can be a little sticky to work with, but rest assured that these bake up beautifully.

1 cup (300 g) mashed banana (from about 2 overly ripe bananas)

1 cup (120 g) sprouted oat flour (see Note on page 41)

¼ cup (65 g) sprouted almond butter, peanut butter or any other nut butter

½ tsp cinnamon (optional)

Preheat the oven to 350°F (175°C). Line a baking sheet with parchment paper or grease it with a healthy fat (ghee, coconut oil, butter) and set aside.

In a large bowl, combine the banana, oat flour, almond butter and cinnamon (if using). Place the batter in the fridge for about 30 minutes to firm up a bit (this makes the batter easier to work with). Use a spoon to scoop small portions of the batter onto the prepared baking sheet. These won't spread or change shape while baking, so form them how you want to eat them.

Bake for 10 to 12 minutes or until lightly golden brown on the bottom. Let the cookies cool on a wire rack.

Serve to your baby whole or let them "gum" or "gnaw" on them. For older toddlers, feel free to add some bittersweet dark chocolate chips and drizzle the finished cookies with more nut butter.

Store in an airtight glass container in the fridge for up to 1 month or freeze for up to 3 months.

Beet & Buckwheat Fritters

Yield: 8 fritters

I love any excuse to add beets to recipes for my family. Not only are they incredibly nourishing, but they turn any dish into a beautiful pink hue (if you use purple beets). These fritters are a great way to add some color to your little one's plate. I love this recipe because you can whip up the batter and store it for up to 3 days in your fridge, so you don't need to make a whole batch at once (though we often do if we're feeding the whole family on a Sunday morning). These taste wonderful with a dollop of plain whole-milk Greek yogurt for some extra protein.

½ cup (60 g) buckwheat flour

½ cup (60 g) millet flour

¾ cup (180 ml) plain whole-milk yogurt

½ tsp baking soda

½ tsp unrefined salt (optional if feeding to a baby under 1)

½ tsp garlic powder

½ tsp onion powder

½ tsp dried rosemary

2 eggs, beaten

¼ cup (60 ml) melted ghee or butter + more for frying

¾ cup (83 g) shredded beets (raw)

The evening before making your fritters, combine the buckwheat and millet flours with the yogurt and cover with a dish towel. Leave in a warm spot in your kitchen overnight (see Note).

The next morning, stir in the baking soda, salt (if using), garlic powder, onion powder and rosemary. The mixture will be "gummy," and that's okay. Add the eggs and melted ghee or butter. Fold in the beets until everything is well combined.

Heat a cast-iron skillet over medium-high heat. Add a nourishing cooking fat like ghee, duck fat or tallow and, once melted, use a ¼-cup (60-ml) measuring cup to spoon in batter. Cook for about 3 minutes per side or until lightly browned and cooked through.

Let the fritters cool a bit on a wire rack before serving.

Serve to your baby whole, or slice into thin strips and let them practice their pincer grasp. Or simply crumble a pancake over some Greek yogurt.

Store in an airtight glass container in the fridge for up to 3 days. Leftovers can be enjoyed cold, or reheated in a 300°F (150°C) oven for 10 to 12 minutes.

Note: If using sprouted flours, you can skip the overnight soaking process.

Veggie-Loaded Turkey Bites

Yield: 18 bites

Not only are these delicious served to anyone of any age, but I love how nutrient dense these are with the mix of protein, vitamins and minerals from both the meat and veggies combined. These freeze really well and are nice to have on hand for daycare lunches or last-minute dinners. You can take a frozen bite out of the freezer, throw it in a lunch box and it will be thawed by lunchtime! These are great eaten warm or at room temperature.

1 lb (454 g) ground turkey

¾ cup (93 g) grated zucchini or summer squash (squeezed of excess moisture in a dish towel)

¾ cup (83 g) grated carrots

½ cup (25 g) very finely chopped Swiss chard (can substitute spinach)

3 green onions, finely chopped (white and pale green parts)

½ tsp dried thyme

½ tsp dried parsley

½ tsp dried oregano

½ tsp unrefined salt (optional if serving to a baby under 1)

Black pepper to taste

Preheat the oven to 350°F (175°C). Grease a baking sheet with a healthy cooking fat (ghee, butter, duck fat) and set aside.

In a large bowl, combine the turkey with the zucchini, carrots, Swiss chard, green onions, thyme, parsley, oregano, salt (if using) and black pepper. Place in the fridge for 30 minutes to firm up a bit (the batter is a tad wet, and this will make it easier to work with). Use a spoon to scoop the mixture into about 2-inch (5-cm) balls and place on the prepared baking sheet.

Bake in the oven until cooked through and golden brown on top, 18 to 22 minutes, or until a thermometer inserted into a meatball registers 165°F (75°C).

Serve to your baby whole, sliced into thin strips or crumbled onto whole milk yogurt.

Store in an airtight glass container in the fridge for up to 4 days.

Note: You can swap turkey for ground chicken or pork.

Part III:

Family Favorites
(1 Year & Beyond)

This part of the book houses some of our most beloved family recipes. However, it took a little patience and creativity to get Pepper to enjoy all the same meals as we do. Remember, when you're still feeding a child under 2, some foods need to be modified and plates and portion sizes will vary from family member to family member. I hope some of the tricks that worked for us will work for you as well!

The Importance of "FFPs"

Most of the recipes in this section I've fit into the "FFP" protocol. FFP stands for fat, fiber and protein. This is something I've learned to strive for when I prepare snacks and meals for my family. The FFP protocol will ensure that your child's blood sugar stays in check and their mood and energy levels will most likely be more consistent. Of course, you won't always be able to follow this when different circumstances arise, but it's a nice thing to keep in the back of your mind when you prepare food for your family. I've seen a big difference in Pepper's energy and mood levels when she's had a meal that incorporates these three things.

Deconstructing the Plate and Small Portions

Early into feeding whole plates of food to Pepper, I made a discovery that I initially thought was a fluke, but it turned out there was a reason behind what was happening. When she was around 16 months old, I noticed that sometimes when I gave her a small bowl of ingredients that had been mixed up to make a meal—like a few bites of chili—she would push it away. But, when I deconstructed it, placing beans over here, meat over there, cheese right here, and so forth, she would go to town, finishing it all and often asking for more.

A similar experience helped me learn that it can be better to serve tiny portions. You can always serve more, but I found that when I gave Pepper a full plate of food, she'd immediately throw it on the ground. Turns out, she was totally overwhelmed with the amount of food. And I quickly realized my portion sizes for her were way off. I had to think tiny, I mean really tiny.

Offering just a small sampling of deconstructed foods often led to her eating and then asking/gesturing for more. It turns out this is a very real stage that a lot of kids go through. Researchers think that psychologically, it's a lot easier for young minds to navigate food when it's segmented and served in small portions. Keeping food in separate piles rather than all mixed up is less overwhelming, which can make them more inclined to eat.

Same foods, just different presentations—and very different results.

The good news is, by parsing the components of a meal, you may still be able to enjoy a family meal together. Your plate will just look different from your kid's.

Try This: Another thing I've learned is the importance of respecting your child's cues. If they are literally pushing food away or don't seem interested in eating, they may not be hungry. If your boxes are checked (small portions, deconstructed food, served with a "safe" food—see page 39) you can try again later. Forcing kids to eat when they're not hungry or interested has proven to backfire and creates a stressful and hostile eating environment. The opposite of this is true, too. If your baby keeps reaching for or asking for more food, let them continue to eat. Babies, toddlers and young children go through so many growth spurts and their hunger levels and appetites vary widely! Trust your kid. They know their body! Of course, there are always exceptions to this, so if you're worried about your child's weight or health, always chat with your healthcare provider.

Condiments to Keep Things Fresh

If you're familiar with my recipes, you already know I'm a big fan of condiments. Pepper is too, and I'm convinced most kids are. I mean, who doesn't like to dip, swirl and liven up their food and the act of mealtime itself?

Take my veggie cheese balls (see recipes on pages 58–61), for example. Pepper used to love them. But when I was photographing this book, she wouldn't touch them. Rather than give up, I decided to serve them a little differently and added some of my homemade Date-Sweetened Ketchup (page 85) in a tiny dish alongside them. All of a sudden, she was into them! The ketchup changes the taste, but it also makes eating them more exciting and fun and turns it into an actual activity.

I'm a big fan of serving things just a little differently to see if you can capture your child's interest, especially when they tire of something they used to like. Months later, "dipping" continues to be one of her favorite ways to enjoy a meal! Below are our two favorite "Pepper-approved" dips, Date-Sweetened Ketchup and Greek Yogurt Ranch.

Greek Yogurt Ranch

Yield: 1 cup (240 ml)

½ cup (120 ml) plain whole-milk Greek yogurt

1 tsp garlic powder

½ tsp onion powder

½ tsp dried dill

½ tsp dried parsley

Pinch of unrefined salt

1½ tsp (8 ml) fresh lemon juice

Add the yogurt, garlic powder, onion powder, dill, parsley, salt and lemon juice to a medium bowl and mix well. If the mixture is too thick, add a touch of water. Taste for seasonings and adjust as needed.

Store in a Mason jar in the fridge for up to 7 days.

Food for Thought: Toddlers are eager to help, so task them with a job. Let them set the table and pick out specific napkins or a special cup they want everyone to drink out of. Give them condiments or salt and pepper to place on the table. I swear, Pepper is a natural born assistant. She is hungry to roll up her sleeves and get the job done. This makes her even more excited to finally sit down to a family meal after she's helped set the stage.

Date-Sweetened Ketchup

Yield: 1 pint (473 ml)

This naturally sweetened ketchup is a Bemis family favorite condiment. I feel good about the ingredients, and sweetening the ketchup with juicy dates makes for an extra nourishing dip that tastes great with everything from burgers to salmon nuggets to roasted veggies and scrambled eggs! Go wild!

½ cup (60 g) tightly packed and chopped pitted Medjool dates (about 5 large dates)

7 oz (198 g) tomato paste (look for tomato paste sold in glass jars if you can)

5 tbsp (75 ml) apple cider vinegar

2 tbsp (30 ml) water

½ tsp unrefined salt

½ tsp onion powder

½ tsp garlic powder

⅛ tsp ground allspice

Pinch of ground cloves

Place the pitted dates in a large bowl and cover with boiling water. Let them soak for about 5 minutes to soften. Drain.

Add the softened dates, tomato paste, vinegar, water, salt, onion powder, garlic powder, allspice and cloves to the bowl of a food processor or blender and mix until smooth. If this mixture is too thick, add a splash more water to thin to your desired consistency. Taste for seasonings and adjust as needed.

Store the ketchup in a glass container in the fridge for up to 3 weeks or freeze for up to 6 months.

Breakfasts

Almond & Oat Pancakes with Stewed Berries

Yield: 4–6 servings (depending on ages and appetites)

These fiber-rich pancakes are one of our favorite weekend breakfasts. Not only do they pack a good nutritional punch, but they're a breeze to whip up in the blender. We like to top our pancakes and berries with Greek yogurt for added nutrients and protein. This is also a great breakfast to have your little one help you prepare because you can pre-measure your ingredients and have them dump everything into the blender and watch it all whirl away!

Almond & Oat Pancakes

¾ cup (71 g) almond flour

¾ cup (90 g) sprouted oat flour (see Note on page 41)

1 tsp ground cinnamon

¼ tsp ground nutmeg

½ tsp baking soda

¼ tsp unrefined salt

2 eggs

¾ cup (180 ml) plain whole-milk Greek yogurt

1 tsp almond extract

Coconut oil or ghee for frying

Greek yogurt (for serving)

Stewed Berries

2 cups (300 g) fresh or frozen berries

½ cup (120 ml) water

½ tsp vanilla extract

Dash of cinnamon

To make the pancakes, place the almond flour, oat flour, cinnamon, nutmeg, baking soda and salt in a blender and process until just combined. Add the eggs, yogurt and almond extract. Blend, stopping to scrape down the sides as needed, until evenly combined.

Heat a large cast-iron skillet over medium-high heat. Add the cooking fat and, once melted, add ¼-cup (60-ml) spoonfuls of the batter to the pan (you should be able to fit about three pancakes at a time). Cook until golden brown on the underside, about 3 minutes. Flip and cook for an additional 2 to 3 minutes or until cooked through.

To prepare the berries, add the berries, water, vanilla and cinnamon to a saucepan over medium-high heat. Bring to a boil, then reduce the heat to medium-low and simmer until the berries thicken and the water evaporates. Use a wooden spoon to mash up the berries a bit.

Serve the pancakes topped with a spoonful of Greek yogurt and the berries.

Store leftover pancakes in a sealed glass container in the fridge for up to 3 days and gently reheat in a 350°F (175°C) oven for 7 to 10 minutes. Store berries in a sealed glass container in the fridge for up to 7 days.

Sprouted Spelt Flour Breakfast Muffins with Sausage & Apple

Yield: 14–16 muffins

These muffins are awesome! They combine sweet and savory flavors beautifully. I love that these muffins are hearty enough to be considered a "mini meal" because they are loaded with essential vitamins, minerals, calcium, probiotics and plenty of protein. The batter makes just over a dozen muffins, and we usually like to make a few "mini pancakes" with the extra batter fried up in a little ghee. It's a fun and tasty way to eat these as well!

2 cups (240 g) sprouted spelt flour (see Note on page 41)

1 tsp baking soda

1 tsp unrefined salt

1 tsp dried thyme

¼ tsp crushed red pepper flakes

¼ tsp ground nutmeg

½ lb (226 g) pork sausage

3 cups (90 g) loosely packed spinach or Swiss chard

1 cup (240 ml) plain whole-milk Greek yogurt

¾ cup (180 ml) unsweetened applesauce

2 eggs, beaten

¼ cup (60 ml) melted ghee

½ cup (57 g) shredded extra-sharp Cheddar cheese

1 cup (125 g) diced apple

Preheat the oven to 350°F (175°C). Grease a standard-sized muffin tin or line with parchment muffin liners.

In a large bowl, combine the flour, baking soda, salt, thyme, red pepper flakes and nutmeg. Set aside.

In a large cast-iron skillet over medium-high heat, add the sausage and cook, using a wooden spoon to break up the meat a bit, until lightly browned and cooked through. Use a slotted spoon to remove the sausage to a paper towel–lined plate. Reserve 1 tablespoon (15 ml) of the drippings in the pan then add the spinach. Cook until wilted, about 2 minutes. Remove the pan from the heat and, when the spinach is cool enough to handle, chop then set aside.

Add the yogurt, applesauce, eggs and melted ghee to the flour and mix well. Fold in the sausage, spinach, Cheddar and apples and mix. Fill the prepared muffin pan with the batter (you may have leftover batter—see the recipe introduction) and bake in the oven until cooked through, 20 to 22 minutes.

Store leftover muffins in the fridge for up to 5 days. Gently reheat before serving.

Food for Thought: Changing up where we ate was a fun thing to do when Pepper began to get a little picky about eating. We often set up a picnic on our living room floor, and she loved inviting her stuffed animals to join us at mealtime. This would usually lead to her eating more food and being really excited about the "new" location!

Muffin Pan Frittata Cups with DIY Toppings

Yield: 12 mini frittatas

This is a fun breakfast that will involve your little ones. Have them choose toppings and keep the toppings in separate small bowls and then let them sprinkle the muffins with the toppings of their choice. This is a "rough" guide, so feel free to swap out any of the veggies, cheeses or meats with whatever you fancy. I love using leftovers for this. The beauty of these frittata cups is how customizable they are! Each of the topping options is enough for four frittata cups.

Base

12 eggs

½ red or yellow onion, finely chopped

Salt and pepper

Salmon & Goat Cheese

¼ cup (60 g) cooked salmon, flaked

¼ cup (15 g) diced mixed herbs (dill, parsley and chives)

A few spears of leftover cooked asparagus, chopped (optional)

A few sprinkles of fresh goat cheese, crumbled

Roasted Red Pepper & Sausage

¼ cup (50 g) finely chopped roasted red peppers (from the jar is just fine)

¼ cup (32 g) cooked and crumbled sausage

¼ cup (28 g) finely grated extra-sharp Cheddar cheese

A sprinkle of chives

Bacon & Potato

¼ cup (36 g) finely chopped cooked bacon

¼ cup (40 g) finely chopped cooked potatoes

¼ cup (28 g) finely grated extra-sharp Cheddar cheese

A sprinkle of chives

Preheat the oven to 350°F (175°C). Grease a standard-sized 12 cup muffin tin and set it aside.

To make the base, in a large bowl, whisk the eggs with the onion, salt and pepper. Pour the mixture evenly among the muffin cups. Sprinkle any of the three topping combinations onto each of the four muffin cups. Bake for 15 to 20 minutes or until set. Let cool slightly and serve warm.

Store in a sealed container in the fridge for up to 4 days.

Food for Thought: Find opportunities to give your child control. Hand them a tiny jar of grated cheese to sprinkle onto their food, or a cup of cream to pour into their oatmeal. Oftentimes, doing this would inspire Pepper to try a bite after she personally added a few garnishes or final touches!

Beet, Banana & Date Bread

Yield: 1 loaf

I love this bread! Not only is it a fun (and pretty) way to add beets to your family's diet, but this loaf is only sweetened with fruit! Between the overripe bananas and dates, this loaf is something I feel pretty darn great about feeding my children. We usually serve this bread toasted, smeared with a little unsalted butter and served alongside some scrambled eggs for a complete breakfast that will not cause a sugar crash. I hope you and your family enjoy this loaf as much as we do!

¾ cup (about 6 oz [90 g]) Medjool dates, pitted

½ cup (120 ml) boiling water

¼ cup (57 g) unsalted butter or ghee at room temperature

2 large eggs, room temperature

2 tsp (10 ml) vanilla extract

2 cups (240 g) sprouted spelt flour (see Note on page 41)

½ tsp unrefined salt

1 tsp baking soda

1 tsp cinnamon

¼ tsp nutmeg

3 large, ripe bananas, mashed

1 cup (110 g) shredded raw beets

Handful of extra dark chocolate chips (optional)

Preheat the oven to 350°F (175°C) and place an oven rack in the upper third of the oven. Grease a 8½ x 4½–inch (22 x 11–cm) loaf pan with butter or ghee (or line it with parchment paper) and set it aside.

Place the dates in a bowl and cover with the boiling water. Allow the dates to soak for 15 minutes. Then, add the dates, along with the soaking water, to the bowl of a food processor. Process until a thick paste forms. Add the butter, eggs and vanilla and process until well blended.

In a large bowl, combine the flour, salt, baking soda, cinnamon and nutmeg and mix with a wooden spoon.

Pour the wet mixture into the bowl with the dry ingredients and mix well. Add the mashed bananas and fold in the beets and chocolate chips (if using).

Pour the mixture into the prepared loaf pan and bake in the oven until cooked through, 55 to 60 minutes (cooking times will vary from kitchen to kitchen, so start checking your loaf often around the 50-minute mark).

Store in an airtight container on the counter for 1 day or in the fridge for 5 days. Slice and lightly toast before serving.

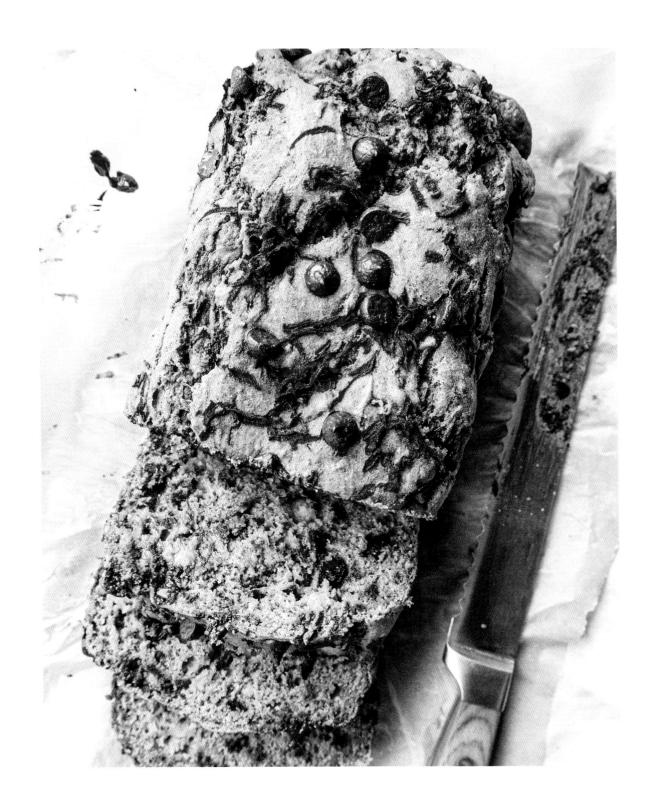

Overnight Porridge with Blueberries & Cardamom

Yield: 4 servings (depending on ages and appetites)

This is a wonderful breakfast to make during the winter months. We use the frozen berries from the summer season and bring them back to life in this simple, nourishing and hearty breakfast. Feel free to add some chopped nuts, a drizzle of nut butter or a dollop of Greek yogurt to add a little more "umph" and protein to this porridge. This is one of Pepper's favorite ways to start the day on a cold January morning.

1½ cups (135 g) old fashioned rolled oats

2 cups (480 ml) warm water

2 tbsp (30 ml) apple cider vinegar or lemon juice

½ tsp unrefined salt

1 tsp ground cardamom

¾ cup (111 g) frozen blueberries

1 large Medjool date, pitted and roughly chopped

1½ tbsp (21 g) unsalted butter

½ cup (120 ml) whole milk

Mix the oats with the warm water and vinegar in a bowl and cover with a kitchen towel. Place in a warm spot for 8 to 24 hours.

In the morning, drain and rinse the oats under cool water.

Bring 1½ cups (360 ml) of water to a boil. Add the soaked oats, salt, cardamom, blueberries and dates. Reduce the heat to low, cover the pot and simmer for 3 to 5 minutes. Remove the pan from the heat, stir in the butter and milk and enjoy.

Store leftovers in the fridge for up to 3 days. Gently reheat on the stove over a double boiler.

Pepper & Maize Frittata

Yield: 1 frittata

This frittata is named for my girls! Pepper is my older daughter and Maize is my youngest. It's one of our favorite summertime breakfasts and is chock full of our favorite summer veggies. Peppers and corn are the heart and soul of this meal, and their flavors meld so beautifully. Not only is the frittata a simple and healthy breakfast, but it can also be served for lunch or dinner with a simple salad. Serve warm, room temperature or chilled.

2 tbsp (28 g) ghee, butter or duck fat

1 small red onion, thinly sliced

1 small red bell pepper, thinly sliced

1 small green bell pepper, thinly sliced

1 small orange bell pepper, thinly sliced

2 cloves garlic, minced

Pinch of crushed red pepper flakes

½ tsp dried oregano

1 cup (154 g) fresh corn kernels (can use frozen if needed)

Salt to taste

8 large eggs

¼ cup (62 g) ricotta cheese

Preheat the oven to 350°F (175°C). Grease a 9-inch (23-cm) pie plate with ghee or duck fat.

In a cast-iron skillet over medium heat, add the cooking fat and, when melted, add the onion, bell peppers, garlic, red pepper flakes and oregano and cook, stirring often, until the vegetables are tender and fragrant, about 8 minutes. Add the corn and cook until the vegetables are tender, about 5 minutes more. Season with salt.

In a bowl, whisk the eggs with a pinch of salt. Add half of the veggies and mix well. Pour the mixture into the prepared pie plate, and top with the remaining veggies. Dollop the ricotta cheese evenly over the top of the frittata. Bake in the oven until set and cooked through, 25 to 30 minutes.

Store leftovers in the fridge for up to 4 days.

Food for Thought: I learned this practice from my research on childhood eating behavior and it really resonated with me. This can be a hard one, though! Try not to react or praise your kids for eating a certain food. If your child finally tries that broccoli on their plate after you've prepared it 30 different times in 30 different ways, don't make a big deal about it. The same is true if they aren't eating something on their plate. Giving too much attention to what is or isn't eaten can backfire. Continue to model the behavior you want to see without praise or punishment. I still ask questions about the food my daughters are eating, such as, "What did that taste like?" and so on, but I do my best to hold back on the praise or pressure to eat food.

Family Dinners

Sheet Pan Cauliflower Nachos

Yield: 4–6 servings (depending on ages and appetites)

This meal is great for the whole family and can easily be "deconstructed" for a toddler who isn't as keen on eating this straight off the sheet pan with the rest of the family. We add leftover shredded chicken to the pan, but this can easily be made vegetarian by leaving out the chicken. Loaded with protein, vitamins and minerals from the veggies, beans and cheese, this is a great weeknight dinner the whole family will enjoy. We make these with our simple homemade Duck-Fat Tortilla Chips (page 132), but feel free to use store bought if you're in a pinch for time.

5 cups (500 g) cauliflower florets (from about 1 large head of cauliflower)

¾ tsp chili powder

¾ tsp ground cumin

½ tsp paprika

½ tsp onion powder

½ tsp garlic powder

¼ tsp unrefined salt

2 tbsp (30 ml) melted ghee or duck fat

2 big handfuls of Duck-Fat Tortilla Chips (page 132)

Preheat the oven to 400°F (205°C). Liberally grease a baking sheet and set it aside.

In a large bowl, toss the cauliflower with the chili powder, cumin, paprika, onion powder, garlic powder, salt and ghee or duck fat. Place the mixture on the prepared baking sheet and roast in the oven until lightly browned and tender, 18 to 20 minutes.

Remove the pan from the oven, push the cauliflower toward the center of the pan, then layer the chips around the edges, using tongs to redistribute the cauliflower over the chips.

(continued)

Sheet Pan Cauliflower Nachos

(continued)

¾ cup (130 g) cooked kidney beans or black beans (if from a can, rinsed and drained)

Handful leftover shredded chicken (optional)

¾ cup (53 g) finely shredded cabbage (purple or green)

¾ cup (85 g) shredded Cheddar or mozzarella (or a combination)

2–3 tbsp (30–45 g) pickled jalapeños (optional)

½ cup (8 g) finely chopped cilantro (for serving)

Diced avocado (for serving)

Plain whole milk yogurt or sour cream (for serving)

Top with the beans, chicken (if using), cabbage, cheese and pickled jalapeños (if using). Place the pan back in the oven and bake until the beans and chicken are heated through and the cheese melts and becomes bubbly, 6 to 8 minutes.

Serve with cilantro, avocado and yogurt. These are best eaten the same day they are made.

Food for Thought: Make it FUN! If your kid is struggling with a meal, see if they wouldn't mind "feeding" you. Sometimes if Pepper seems uninterested in eating but I know she's hungry, I'll ask if she could feed me a few bites of food. We'll laugh and I'll exaggerate my chewing and swallowing. She'll usually get a kick out of this and then start feeding herself. Another great trick for this is to bring her favorite stuffed animal to the table. "Bear" often joins us at mealtimes and, if she gives him a few bites of fish, she'll usually start feeding herself, too.

Pumpkin Chili

Yield: 6–8 servings (depending on ages and appetites)

We make this chili every Halloween and then at least twice a month throughout the winter. Now that we have a toddler to feed, this has become an even more fun chili to make for the family. The toppings are part of the fun when it comes to chili night. Go wild and use any toppings you wish. Avocado, radishes and green or red onions would all be nice. We usually serve ours with whole-milk plain yogurt, grated cheese and homemade Duck-Fat Tortilla Chips (page 132) for dipping! When Pepper first started eating chili, she preferred hers "deconstructed." Now that she's older, she loves her bowl of chili stirred all together. And the chips, oh yeah, she can't get enough!

1 (2-lb [907-g]) sugar pumpkin or any winter squash, such as butternut, Hubbard, acorn or delicata

2 tbsp (28 g) ghee or duck fat, divided

1¾ cups (420 ml) water, divided

1 lb (454 g) ground beef

Preheat the oven to 400°F (205°C).

Slice the pumpkin in half or into quarters. Scoop out the seeds. Melt 1 tablespoon (14 g) of the ghee or duck fat and brush it on the flesh of the pumpkin. Place the pumpkin halves, cut-side down, on a rimmed baking sheet and drizzle in ¼ cup (60 ml) of the water. Roast in the oven until the pumpkin is fork tender, about 45 minutes. Remove the pan from the oven and, when cool enough to handle, scoop out the flesh and mash or puree it with an immersion blender or food processor.

While the pumpkin cooks, start the chili. Heat a large Dutch oven over medium-high heat. Add the ground beef and use a wooden spoon to break up the meat a bit. Cook until the meat is no longer pink and lightly browned, about 8 minutes. With a slotted spoon, remove the meat to a large plate or bowl.

(continued)

Pumpkin Chili

(continued)

---

1 large yellow onion, finely chopped

1 large bell pepper (any color), seeded and roughly chopped

3 cloves garlic, finely chopped

1 tbsp (8 g) chili powder

1 tsp ground cumin

1 tsp ground cinnamon

2 tsp (4 g) cocoa powder (this makes it rich and oh so delicious!)

Hefty pinch of unrefined salt and pepper

2 tbsp (32 g) tomato paste

1 (28-oz [794-g]) jar crushed tomatoes, with their juices

1½ cups (266 g) cooked kidney beans (if from a can, rinsed and drained)

Plain whole-milk yogurt or sour cream (for serving)

Shredded Cheddar cheese (for serving)

Homemade Duck-Fat Tortilla Chips (page 132; for serving)

Avocado slices (for serving)

Add the remaining 1 tablespoon (14 g) of ghee or duck fat to the pan and add the onion and bell pepper. Cook, stirring occasionally until softened, about 5 minutes. Add the garlic, chili powder, cumin, cinnamon, cocoa powder, salt and pepper. Cook for 1 minute longer. Add the tomato paste and stir the veggies, coating them in the tomato paste and spices. Pour in the jar of tomatoes, 1½ cups (368 g) of the cooked pumpkin puree and the kidney beans. Add the remaining 1½ cups (360 ml) of water and bring to a boil. Reduce the heat to low and return the meat back to the pot. Simmer the chili for 30 minutes.

Serve with yogurt or sour cream, Cheddar cheese, tortilla chips and avocado slices.

Store leftovers in an airtight glass container in the fridge for up to 4 days or freeze for up to 3 months.

Chicken & Stars Soup

Yield: 6–8 servings (depending on ages and appetites)

I am a child of the '80s and grew up eating Campbell's Chicken & Stars soup. It was a childhood favorite (especially when we were fighting a cough or cold). I love this more nourishing version that doesn't come from a can and is loaded with farm-fresh ingredients. Local chicken and veggies are the backbone of this soup, and the veggie cut-out stars take this over the top. I will admit, cutting out the stars is a little time consuming, but it's a great activity for an older toddler (3+). And younger toddlers can watch you cut them and help put them in a bowl to the side for you. Aside from cutting out the stars, this soup comes together quickly. You can purchase the small, star-shaped metal cookie cutters online for less than $10. However, if you simply want to make this soup sans the star shape, you can call this "Full Moon Chicken Soup" and keep the carrot slices in rounds.

2 large carrots

2 tbsp (28 g) ghee, butter or duck fat

2 stalks celery, finely chopped

1 large yellow onion, finely chopped

2 large cloves garlic, finely chopped

2 tsp (2 g) dried thyme

Tiny pinch of crushed red pepper flakes (omit if your child is extremely sensitive to spice)

Salt and pepper to taste

4 cups (960 ml) homemade broth (or low sodium chicken broth)

4 cups (960 ml) water

1¼ lb (567 g) boneless, skinless chicken breasts

2 bay leaves

6 oz (170 g) whole-wheat pasta (sprouted if possible)

Grab your toddler and star-shaped cookie cutters. Slice the carrots into thin rounds. Then press the cookie cutter down into the slices to cut into star shapes. You do need to put a little muscle into it so, if you are doing this with younger kids, have them watch you and then take the cut-outs and place them in a bowl to the side.

Heat the ghee in a large Dutch oven over medium-high heat. Add the celery, onion, garlic, carrots, dried thyme, pepper flakes and a fat pinch of salt and pepper. Sauté until the veggies begin to soften, about 5 minutes.

Pour in the broth and water. Add the chicken and bay leaves. Bring to a boil. Reduce the heat and simmer until the chicken is cooked through, 10 to 12 minutes. Remove the chicken from the pot with tongs and, when cool enough to handle, use two forks to shred or chop it into small chunks. Return the chicken to the pot and keep on low heat.

While the soup simmers, cook the pasta according to package directions. Drain the pasta and then add the cooked pasta to the soup. Stir through and let the soup sit another 5 to 8 minutes to let the pasta soak up all the flavors. Remove the bay leaves and serve warm.

Store leftovers in an airtight glass container in the fridge for up to 4 days or freeze for up to 3 months.

Sheet Pan Burgers with Sweet Potato Tater Tots

Yield: 4–6 servings (depending on ages and appetites)

Okay, so I know the best part of a sheet pan meal is that you literally just throw everything on there without much prep work. However, in this case, you do need to prepare the tater tots beforehand. The tater tots are a fun thing to have your toddler help prep, so grab a chair, roll up your toddler's sleeves and let them get a little messy with you!

1 large sweet potato (about 1 lb [454 g]), peeled

1 tbsp (14 g) ghee

1 large egg, lightly beaten

½ cup (45 g) almond flour (or sourdough breadcrumbs)

2 tbsp (10 g) nutritional yeast

½ tsp garlic powder

½ tsp onion powder

½ tsp smoked paprika

½ tsp salt

1 lb (454 g) ground beef (preferably grass-fed and finished)

½ large yellow onion, thinly sliced

1 tbsp (15 ml) melted ghee

Preheat the oven to 400°F (205°C) and place oven racks in the upper and lower third of the oven. Liberally grease two baking sheets with ghee and set to the side.

Finely grate the sweet potato on the large holes of a box grater or using the grater attachment on a food processor.

Heat the ghee in a large cast-iron skillet over medium heat. Add the grated sweet potato and cook, stirring occasionally, for 3 to 5 minutes, or until softened. Remove from the heat.

Add the sweet potatoes to a large bowl and add the egg, almond flour, nutritional yeast, garlic powder, onion powder, paprika and salt. Stir with a wooden spoon until well combined.

Using your hands, gently form the sweet potato mixture into tablespoon-sized (15-g) rectangles (the mixture will be wet, but that's okay—these don't have to be perfectly shaped). Space them out evenly on the baking sheet and place in the upper rack of the oven for 10 minutes.

While the sweet potatoes are cooking for the first 10 minutes, form the burgers. Make about ½-inch (1.3-cm)–thick patties and then place them on the other prepared baking sheet. Add the sliced onions to the same sheet pan and drizzle them with a little melted ghee.

(continued)

Sheet Pan Burgers with Sweet Potato Tater Tots

(continued)

Thinly sliced Cheddar cheese for each burger (or your favorite cheese)

Homemade Date-Sweetened Ketchup (page 85) and mayo (for serving)

Remove the pan with the tater tots from the oven and use a thin metal spatula to gently flip the tater tots. Return the pan to the bottom rack of the oven, and place the burgers on the upper rack. Bake for 10 minutes, then remove the burgers from the oven, put the onions on top of the burgers then top with the cheese. Place back in the oven for 2 to 3 minutes longer or until the cheese has melted, the burgers are cooked through and the sweet potato tots are golden brown.

Serve burgers open face with date-sweetened ketchup, mayo and a bun if desired.

Store leftover burgers and tots in the refrigerator for up to 3 days. Gently reheat in a 350°F (175°C) oven for 10 to 12 minutes.

Food For Thought: I was on the fast track to becoming a short-order cook when Pepper was around 2 years old. She began to eat less at mealtimes and then would ask me to make her a snack 30 minutes later. This inspired me to start a new approach. Instead of pressuring her to eat the food on her plate at mealtime, I would just let her know that the kitchen was closed and wouldn't open up again until the next meal. I would leave out the plate of food that was already made for an hour after dinner and she would usually come back to eat it. If you're struggling with the same situation, I hope this helps!

Sheet Pan Butternut Squash & Black Bean Tacos with Lime Crema Sauce

Yield: 4–6 servings (depending on ages and appetites)

This is such a fun meal to make with toddlers and young kids. Everyone can take charge and assemble their own tacos with toppings they love. Pepper usually goes extra heavy on the beans and avocado and she likes to "dip" her veggies into the sauce rather than have it drizzled on her taco. The sauce is easy to whip up, and I think it really takes these tacos over the top. You'll find many uses for it, and don't be scared by the spices. It's not overly spicy, and I think your little ones will enjoy it too! We love to serve these tacos with our homemade Duck-Fat Tortilla Chips (page 132).

Tacos

5 cups (700 g) chopped (1-inch [2.5-cm] cubes) butternut squash

½ tsp chili powder

½ tsp ground cumin

½ tsp paprika

½ tsp garlic powder

¼ tsp unrefined salt

1–2 tbsp (15–30 ml) melted ghee

1 medium yellow onion, thinly sliced

2 cups (344 g) cooked black beans (if from a can, rinsed and drained)

1 cup (154 g) corn kernels (if frozen, thawed)

Corn tortillas (for serving)

Preheat the oven to 425°F (220°C) and lightly grease a baking sheet with ghee or butter.

Toss the butternut squash with the chili powder, cumin, paprika, garlic powder and salt and drizzle with the melted ghee. Spread on the prepared baking sheet and roast in the oven for 15 minutes.

Remove the pan from the oven, add the thinly sliced onion and give everything a good toss. Return the pan to the oven and cook for about 15 more minutes, or until the squash is golden brown and the onion is tender.

Remove the pan from the oven and scatter the beans and corn over the vegetables. Place the pan back in the oven until just warmed through, about 5 minutes. (At this point you can wrap the tortillas in a damp dish towel and place them in the oven for 5 minutes to warm through if you wish.)

(continued)

Sheet Pan Butternut Squash & Black Bean Tacos with Lime Crema Sauce

(continued)

Lime Crema Sauce

½ cup (120 ml) plain whole-milk Greek yogurt

1 tbsp (15 ml) fresh lime juice

¼ tsp lime zest

½ tsp chili powder

¼ tsp paprika

⅛ tsp ground cumin

Tiny pinch of cayenne pepper (optional)

Pinch of salt

Optional Toppings

Avocado

Cilantro

Pickled jalapeños

Shredded cabbage

While the veggies cook, prepare the sauce. Whisk the yogurt, lime juice and zest, chili powder, paprika, cumin, cayenne (if using) and salt in a bowl until well incorporated. Taste for seasonings and adjust as needed.

Serve the tacos family style with your favorite toppings and the Lime Crema Sauce in bowls on the side of the sheet pan.

Store leftover veggies in an airtight glass container in the fridge for up to 4 days.

Food for Thought: Get your kids helping!! Have them chop, stir or serve themselves their own food. When kids participate in the preparation of mealtime, they'll be more inclined to try the food. Pepper has become such an eager little helper in the kitchen. It took some time, but the extra messes were worth every moment of spending time in the kitchen together. And rest assured, the messes will get less "messy" with more practice and patience.

Muffin Pan Meatloaves

Yield: 12 mini meatloaves

I don't think I'll go back to making meatloaf in a loaf pan again! These mini meatloaves are awesome. Not only are they a fun, individual little meal, but they cook up in half the time so dinner can be on the table in no time when you've got hungry little mouths to feed. Loaded with iron, protein, vitamin B12 and zinc (among others), these are simple and nourishing little bites. Sometimes I'll add a cup of shredded carrots or zucchini, but this is my standard recipe. Feel free to play with it—the homemade ketchup should not be passed up!

1½ lb (680 g) ground beef

1 tbsp (14 g) ghee

½ small red or yellow onion, minced

2 large cloves garlic, minced

1 large egg, lightly beaten

½ cup + 3 tbsp (165 ml) Date-Sweetened Ketchup (page 85), divided

¾ tsp salt

1 tsp dried oregano

½ tsp dried thyme

⅓ cup (32 g) almond flour or super-fine sourdough breadcrumbs

Preheat the oven to 350°F (175°C). Grease a standard 12 cup muffin tin with ghee or butter and set aside.

Add the beef to a large bowl and set aside.

Heat the ghee in a medium cast-iron skillet over medium-high heat and add the onion. Cook, stirring occasionally, until softened and fragrant, about 5 minutes. Add the garlic and cook for 1 minute longer. Add the onion/garlic mixture to the beef and mix well. Add the egg, 3 tablespoons (45 ml) of the Date-Sweetened Ketchup, salt, oregano, thyme and almond flour or breadcrumbs. Mix.

Spoon the mixture into the prepared muffin pan, patting it down firmly into each cup. Bake in the oven for 15 minutes. Remove the pan from the oven, and use the remaining ½ cup (120 ml) of the Date-Sweetened Ketchup to top each muffin, then return the pan to the oven for 10 minutes longer or until the meatloaf is cooked through and an instant-read thermometer registers 160°F (70°C).

Store leftovers in an airtight glass container in the fridge for up to 3 days.

Nourishing Beef Stew

Yield: 4–6 servings (depending on ages and appetites)

There is something incredibly special about a bowl of beef stew. When the first kiss of chilly air creeps onto the farm in the fall, I turn to this recipe. I love how many nourishing ingredients you can pack into this humble stew. We make ours with homemade beef bone broth for a richer, more nutrient-dense stew. However, store-bought low-sodium beef broth is a fine substitution. This meal is always a crowd pleaser and, after prepping all the ingredients, you pretty much let this simmer all day long. Have your kiddos join you at the farmers market to pick out their veggies. This soup feels like a cozy hug and will nourish you and your little ones from the inside out.

¼ cup + 1 tbsp (39 g) sprouted flour (spelt, all-purpose or whole wheat all work), divided

Salt and pepper

2½ lb (1.1 kg) beef stew meat, cubed

3 tbsp (42 g) ghee or beef tallow (or substitute butter)

1 medium onion, finely chopped (red or yellow)

1½ tbsp (24 g) tomato paste

1 tbsp (15 ml) red wine vinegar

4 cups (960 ml) low-salt beef bone broth (homemade preferred)

2 bay leaves

3 fresh thyme sprigs

2 celery stalks, cut into ¼-inch (6-mm) pieces

2 medium carrots, cut into ¼-inch (6-mm) pieces

2 medium parsnips, peeled and cut into ¼-inch (6-mm) pieces

4 medium potatoes (about 1 lb [454 g]), cut into ¼-inch (6-mm) pieces

Place ¼ cup (31 g) of the flour, a fat pinch of salt and pepper in a large bowl and whisk to combine. Place the meat in the flour mixture and toss to coat. Set aside.

In a large Dutch oven over medium heat, melt the ghee. Shake off the excess flour from about one third of the meat and add it to the pot. Cook, stirring occasionally, until the meat browns all over, 4 to 5 minutes. Transfer to a large bowl and repeat with the remaining meat in two batches, adding both batches to the large bowl.

Add the onion to the pot and season with salt and pepper. Cook, stirring occasionally, until softened and fragrant, about 5 minutes. Add the tomato paste, stirring to coat the onion, and continue to cook for 1 minute longer. Add the remaining 1 tablespoon (8 g) of flour and stir to coat the onion. Return the beef to the pot along with any accumulated juices. Add the red wine vinegar, beef bone broth, bay leaves and thyme sprigs and bring to a boil. Reduce the heat to low and simmer, uncovered, for 1½ hours.

Stir in the celery, carrots, parsnips and potatoes and simmer for an additional 30 to 40 minutes, or until the veggies are tender but not falling apart.

Remove from the heat and discard the bay leaves and thyme sprigs. Season to taste with additional salt and pepper.

Store leftovers in an airtight glass container in the fridge for up to 4 days or freeze for up to 3 months.

Penne with Creamy Pumpkin Sauce

Yield: 4–6 servings (depending on ages and appetites)

This pasta is reminiscent of macaroni and cheese. Okay, so maybe not quite as "cheesy" tasting, but the cream sauce is rich and decadent and I'm really pleased with how tasty it is. Pepper calls this pumpkin pasta and usually licks the blender bowl after I make the sauce. The sauce is made with a combination of soaked cashews and roasted pumpkin simply whizzed together with the rest of the ingredients in a blender. You can roast your pumpkin in advance to save time, but honestly, most of this recipe is hands-off time and comes together without much effort (thanks to a high-speed blender!). Sometimes we add cooked chicken or sausage to this pasta, but it tastes great as is. And bonus, leftover sauce tastes great as a dip or drizzled onto roasted veggies.

1 medium-sized sugar pumpkin or butternut squash, sliced in half, seeds removed

1–2 tbsp (15–30 ml) melted ghee or duck fat

1 cup (146 g) raw cashews, soaked for 4 hours (or quick soaked for 30 minutes in boiling water)

2 tbsp (10 g) nutritional yeast

½ tsp smoked paprika

½ tsp onion powder

½ tsp garlic powder

¼ tsp unrefined salt

Juice of half a lemon (about 1 tbsp [15 ml])

1 lb (454 g) whole-wheat sprouted penne pasta; regular pasta works fine too

1 (12-oz [340-g]) bag frozen peas

Leftover cooked shredded chicken, ground turkey or pork for added protein (optional)

Preheat the oven to 400°F (205°C).

Drizzle the pumpkin or squash halves with the melted ghee or oil and place, cut-side down, on a rimmed baking sheet. Drizzle in about ¼ cup (60 ml) of water and place the pan in the oven. Roast until the squash is tender, about 45 minutes.

Drain the soaked cashews and rinse them under cold water.

When the cooked pumpkin or squash is cool enough to handle, scoop out 1½ cups (310 g) of pumpkin and place it in a high-speed blender along with the drained cashews, nutritional yeast, paprika, onion powder, garlic powder, salt, lemon juice and 1½ cups (360 ml) of water. Blend on high for about 45 seconds, stopping to scrape down the sides as you go. If the sauce is too thick, add up to another ½ cup (120 ml) of water to thin as needed. Taste for seasonings and adjust to your liking.

Cook the pasta according to package directions. When there are 2 minutes left of cooking time, add the frozen peas to the pot. Drain the pasta and peas and return them to the pot. Drizzle in half of the pumpkin sauce and give it a good toss. Add your protein of choice (if using) and more sauce to taste.

Keep extra sauce in an airtight container in the fridge for up to 4 days, and store any leftover pasta in the fridge for up to 3 days.

Autumn-Spiced Spaghetti & Meatballs

Yield: 4–6 servings (depending on ages and appetites)

This meal quickly became a Tumbleweed Farm family favorite meal last fall. When the first kiss of chilly air creeps in, and Pepper is changing out of her dirt-covered overalls and slipping into a sweatshirt and fleece pants for the evening, this is the meal I crave. The meatballs are tender and juicy thanks to the addition of roasted pumpkin puree, and the spaghetti is tossed in a lovely creamy tomato sauce that is spiced with cinnamon and sage, which makes this meal feel like the biggest bowl of comfort food. I love this autumn twist on a classic recipe. It's the kind of meal that you think about days after you eat it. I hope you and your family love this recipe as much as we do!

Tomato–Sage Sauce

1 (24-oz [680-g]) jar diced tomatoes with their juices

2 cups (480 ml) low-sodium vegetable stock

2 cups (490 g) roasted pumpkin puree (or any roasted winter squash puree)

1½ tsp (1 g) dried sage

1 tsp ground cinnamon

1 tsp garlic powder

Salt and pepper to taste

Spaghetti & Meatballs

1 lb (454 g) whole-wheat spaghetti (sprouted noodles if you can find them)

Olive oil

1 batch Pumpkin Meatballs (page 54)

Sourdough bread (optional)

To prepare the Tomato–Sage Sauce, add the tomatoes, vegetable stock, pumpkin puree, sage, cinnamon, garlic powder and salt and pepper to a medium saucepan over medium-high heat and bring to a boil. Reduce the heat to medium-low and simmer for 20 minutes, stirring occasionally. Taste for seasonings and adjust as needed. The longer this simmers, the more flavorful it becomes!

Cook the pasta until al dente. Drain the noodles and return them to the pan and toss them in a bit of olive oil.

Add the meatballs and pour in the Tomato–Sage Sauce.

If need be, you can deconstruct this meal to accommodate a young eater. Serve the noodles, meatballs and sauce separately on a plate and let them dip the individual ingredients in the sauce or whatever they fancy!

Serve warm, with a glass of milk and a few hunks of sourdough bread, if desired.

Store leftovers in an airtight glass container in the fridge for up to 4 days.

Creamy Tomato Soup with Cheese Star Biscuits

Yield: 4–6 servings (depending on ages and appetites), with 12 biscuits

This is a lovely soup that can be prepared in no time! Not only is this a simple and tasty soup, but it packs a lot of nutrition into each spoonful. Tomatoes contain the antioxidant lycopene, which has been linked to many health benefits, including a reduced risk of heart disease and cancer. The creaminess in this soup comes from protein and fiber–rich chickpeas for another nutritional boost. Most tomato soups call for adding a touch of sugar to round out the acidity and balance the flavors; in this version we use a single Medjool date. It adds just a hint of sweetness and balances out the acidity perfectly. Serve this soup warm with cheese star biscuits for dunking. This honestly might become your kiddos' new favorite weeknight dinner!

Creamy Tomato Soup

2 tbsp (28 g) ghee or unsalted butter

1 large yellow onion, finely chopped

3 cloves garlic, minced

2 tsp (2 g) dried thyme

¼ tsp crushed red pepper flakes

½ tsp unrefined salt

Fresh ground black pepper

2 tbsp (32 g) tomato paste

1 (28-oz [794-g]) jar diced tomatoes (with their juices)

1 Medjool date, pitted and chopped

1½ cups (360 ml) low-salt chicken bone broth (or water)

1½ cups (246 g) cooked chickpeas (if from the can, rinsed and drained)

½ cup (120 ml) heavy cream

To make the Creamy Tomato Soup, in a large Dutch oven over medium heat, melt the ghee. Add the onion and cook, stirring often, until lightly browned and fragrant, about 5 minutes. Stir in the garlic, thyme, red pepper flakes, salt, a pinch of pepper and tomato paste and continue to cook for about 1 minute longer, stirring the mixture to coat everything with the tomato paste. Add the tomatoes, date and chicken broth and bring to a boil. Reduce the heat to low, add the chickpeas and simmer for 20 minutes.

Working in batches, carefully puree the soup until smooth. Return to the pot, turn the heat to low and stir in the cream. Taste for seasonings and adjust as needed. This soup gets better with time, so feel free to keep it on low for a while.

While the soup is simmering, prepare the Cheese Star Biscuits.

Preheat the oven to 350°F (175°C). Sprinkle a piece of parchment paper with flour and set aside. Line a baking sheet with another sheet of parchment paper and set aside.

(continued)

Creamy Tomato Soup with Cheese Star Biscuits

(continued)

Cheese Star Biscuits

1½ cups (180 g) sprouted spelt flour, plus more for rolling

¾ tsp baking soda

½ cup (120 ml) plain whole-milk yogurt

1 cup (113 g) shredded Cheddar cheese

¼ cup (57 g) cold, unsalted butter diced

Place the flour, baking soda, yogurt, Cheddar and butter in a food processor and pulse until the dough comes together.

Remove the dough from the processor and form it into a disk. Place the dough on the floured parchment paper. Using a lightly floured rolling pin, roll the dough out until it's about ½ inch (1.3 cm) thick. Using a star cutout, cut individual biscuits. Reroll the dough as needed and cut out more stars until no dough is left. Place the biscuits on the parchment-lined baking sheet and bake in the oven until cooked through and golden brown, 14 to 18 minutes.

Serve the soup topped with the star biscuits.

Store leftovers in an airtight glass container in the fridge for up to 4 days or freeze for up to 3 months. Store leftover biscuits in a glass or stainless-steel container at room temperature for up to 2 days or refrigerate for up to 4 days.

Snacks!

I learned the hard way that "oversnacking" Pepper during the day led to hardly any appetite at dinnertime. It was a hard cycle to break because she got in the habit of "grazing" throughout the day, and I just gave in to her requests. However, after a week of really limiting snacks, she began to eat most of her calories from actual meals.

Snacks should be served intentionally and not in excess. I have a friend that doesn't serve snacks at all and she swears it's the only reason her girls actually eat full meals. We still love snacks around here, but I do believe that if your child comes to a meal actually hungry, they'll be more likely to eat and enjoy the food on their plate (even new or often "disliked" foods can be enjoyed when a kid is actually hungry!). With all that being said, the recipes that follow are all wonderful additions to school lunches, as they are easy to pack and would complement a variety of meals.

Veggie Crackers 3 Ways—Beet, Carrot & Kale

These veggie crackers are AWESOME!! They are superior to store-bought crackers and, as a bonus, they last up to 7 days in a sealed container. We rotate among them, but if there is one that we make more often than the others it's the Beet Buckwheat Crackers! They are so delicious and the bright pink color is Pepper's favorite part. Serve with sliced cheese, hummus or sliced turkey for a nourishing and complete snack.

Beet Buckwheat Crackers

Yield: 50 crackers

---

1 cup (95 g) almond flour (or hazelnut flour)

½ cup (60 g) sprouted buckwheat flour (see Note on page 41)

½ cup (46 g) sprouted chickpea flour (see Note on page 41)

¾ tsp unrefined salt

½ tsp garlic powder

½ tsp onion powder

2 tsp (2 g) dried rosemary

6 tbsp (90 ml) olive oil

1 cup (110 g) shredded raw beets

Preheat the oven to 350°F (175°C) and place an oven rack in the upper third of the oven.

Add the almond flour, buckwheat flour, chickpea flour, salt, garlic powder, onion powder and rosemary to the bowl of a food processor and pulse a few times. Drizzle in the olive oil and pulse a few more times. Add the shredded beets and process until a dough ball forms. This takes a minute or two. If the mixture is too dry, add a touch more oil until you have a workable dough.

Divide the dough in half and place one half of the dough between two large pieces of parchment paper. Use a rolling pin to roll the dough into a thin rectangle (about ⅛ inch [3 mm] thick). Try to keep the thickness even (this will make for even baking).

Remove the top layer of the parchment paper and use a pizza cutter to cut the dough into uniform cracker shapes. There is no need to separate the crackers yet; they will break apart easily after baking! Carefully lift the parchment paper (with the dough still on it) and place it on a baking sheet. Repeat this process with the second ball of dough.

Place both baking sheets in the oven side by side and bake until the edges are lightly browned, 15 to 20 minutes. Cooking times will vary depending on the thickness of your crackers, so start checking your crackers around the 12-minute mark. If the outer crackers start browning faster than the inner crackers, you can use a metal spatula to remove them first, then return the pan to the oven to finish baking the rest.

Remove the pans from the oven and turn the oven down to 200°F (95°C). When the oven has cooled down, place the trays back in the oven to completely dry out and crisp up the crackers. This will take about 2½ to 3 hours (timing will depend on the thickness of your crackers). You will know the crackers are done when they are crispy and break apart easily.

Store in an airtight glass or stainless-steel container for up to 7 days.

Carrot Turmeric Crackers

Yield: 50 crackers

1 cup (95 g) almond flour (or hazelnut flour)

½ cup (60 g) buckwheat flour (sprouted if possible)

½ cup (46 g) chickpea flour (sprouted if possible; see Note on page 41)

¾ tsp unrefined salt

¾ tsp ground turmeric

¾ tsp paprika

½ tsp garlic powder

½ tsp onion powder

2 tbsp (10 g) nutritional yeast (optional)

6 tbsp (90 ml) olive oil

1 cup (110 g) shredded raw carrots

Preheat the oven to 350°F (175°C) and place an oven rack in the upper third of the oven.

Add the almond flour, buckwheat flour, chickpea flour, salt, turmeric, paprika, garlic powder, onion powder and nutritional yeast (if using) to the bowl of a food processor and pulse a few times. Drizzle in the olive oil and pulse a few more times. Add the shredded carrots and process until a dough ball forms. This will take a minute or two. If the mixture is too dry, add a touch more oil until you have a workable dough.

Divide the dough in half and place one half of the dough between two large pieces of parchment paper. Use a rolling pin to roll the dough out until it is about ⅛ inch (3 mm) thick. Try to keep the thickness even (this will make for even baking).

Remove the top layer of the parchment paper and use a pizza cutter to cut the dough into uniform cracker shapes. There is no need to separate the crackers yet; they will break apart easily after baking! Carefully lift the parchment paper (with the dough still on it) and place it on a baking sheet. Repeat this process with the second ball of dough.

Place the baking sheets side by side in the oven and bake until the edges are lightly browned, 15 to 20 minutes. Cooking times will vary depending on the thickness of your crackers, so start checking your crackers around the 12-minute mark. If the outer crackers start browning faster than the inner crackers, you can remove them with a metal spatula first, then return the pan to the oven to finish baking the rest.

Remove the pans from the oven and turn the oven down to 200°F (95°C). When the oven has cooled down, place the trays back in the oven to completely dry out and crisp up the crackers. This will take about 2½ to 3 hours (timing will depend on the thickness of your crackers). You will know the crackers are done when they are crispy and break apart easily.

Store in an airtight container at room temperature for up to 7 days.

Cheddar Kale Crackers

Yield: 50 crackers

½ cup (34 g) roughly chopped kale

1 cup (95 g) almond flour

½ cup (60 g) sprouted buckwheat flour (see Note on page 41)

½ cup (46 g) sprouted chickpea flour (see Note on page 41)

½ tsp unrefined salt

½ tsp garlic powder

½ tsp onion powder

½ tsp paprika

4 oz (113 g) room-temperature butter

1 cup (113 g) freshly grated extra-sharp Cheddar cheese

Preheat the oven to 350°F (175°C) and place an oven rack in the upper third of the oven.

Add the kale to the bowl of a food processor and pulse until very finely chopped. Remove the kale from the processor and place it in a kitchen towel and ring out any extra moisture. Wipe the food processor out with a dry towel to remove extra moisture.

Add the almond flour, buckwheat flour, chickpea flour, salt, garlic powder, onion powder, paprika, butter and cheese to the food processor and process until a ball of dough forms. Add the kale and process until it is well distributed. Divide the dough in half and place one half of dough between two large pieces of parchment paper. Use a rolling pin to roll the dough out into a thin rectangle, about ⅛ inch (3 mm) thick. Try to keep the thickness even (this will make for even baking).

Remove the top layer of the parchment paper and use a pizza cutter to cut the dough into uniform cracker shapes. There is no need to separate the crackers yet; they will break apart easily after baking! Carefully lift the parchment paper (with the dough still on it) and place it on a baking sheet. Repeat this process with the second ball of dough.

Place the baking sheets side by side in the oven and bake until the edges are lightly browned, 15 to 20 minutes. Cooking times will vary depending on the thickness of your crackers, so start checking your crackers around the 12-minute mark. If the outer crackers start browning faster than the inner crackers, you can remove them with a metal spatula first, then return the pan to the oven to finish baking the rest.

Remove the pans from the oven and turn the oven down to 200°F (95°C). When the oven has cooled down, place the trays back in the oven to completely dry out and crisp up the crackers. This will take about 2½ to 3 hours (timing will depend on the thickness of your crackers). You will know the crackers are done when they are crispy and break apart easily.

Store in an airtight container at room temperature for up to 7 days.

Goldfish Crackers

Yield: 80 crackers

When I saw the ingredient list of one of my favorite childhood crackers, my heart sank. The ingredients made me uncomfortable, and I knew they wouldn't be a snack I'd be purchasing for my kids. However, this gave me a fun opportunity to play around in the kitchen and create a more wholesome cracker. And yes, I did purchase a $10 goldfish cutout online (there are many available if you search; mine is from Etsy). I think I nailed these crackers, and they ended up being really easy to prepare! And hey, if you don't want to buy a goldfish cutout, you can simply use a pizza cutter to cut these into regular cracker shapes. These get their "cheesy" color from a dash of turmeric. No artificial coloring needed!

¾ cup (90 g) sprouted spelt flour (see Note on page 41), plus more for cutting the dough

4 tbsp (57 g) unsalted butter

1 cup (113 g) shredded extra-sharp Cheddar cheese

¼ tsp unrefined salt

½ tsp onion powder

½ tsp turmeric

½ tsp paprika

Preheat the oven to 350°F (175°C). Set an oven rack in the upper third of the oven. Line a baking sheet with parchment paper.

Place the spelt flour, butter, Cheddar, salt, onion powder, turmeric and paprika in a food processor and process until a dough ball forms, about 2 minutes.

If the dough feels too soft to work with, place it in the fridge for 25 minutes to firm up a bit. Place the dough in between two sheets of parchment paper and use a rolling pin to roll the dough into a thin rectangle, about ⅛ inch (3 mm) thick. Dip a goldfish cutout (if using) into some flour (this will help ensure a clean cut) and use it to cut shapes from the dough, continuing to dust the cutout with more flour as needed.

Place the crackers on the parchment-lined baking sheet. Repeat until all the dough is used. Place the baking sheet in the oven and bake until the crackers are golden brown and crisp, 15 to 20 minutes. Remove the baking sheet from the oven and reduce the temperature to 200°F (95°C). When the oven has cooled down, place the tray back in the oven for 1 to 2 hours for the crackers to completely dry out.

Store in an airtight glass container for up to 5 days.

Maple Graham Crackers

Yield: 12 servings

These crackers are fun to make with your little kitchen helper. Pepper loves to use a fork to make the trademark graham cracker indentations. Homemade graham crackers will become your new favorite snack to serve with your go-to nut butter. And s'mores night? It just got a little more homemade! I just need to perfect my marshmallow recipe (that's for another book, I guess!).

1 cup (95 g) almond flour (or hazelnut flour)

½ cup (60 g) buckwheat flour (see Note on page 41)

½ cup (46 g) chickpea flour (see Note on page 41)

½ tsp unrefined salt

½ tsp cinnamon

¼ tsp nutmeg

5 tbsp (75 ml) melted butter

¼ cup (60 ml) maple syrup

1 tsp pure vanilla extract

1 tsp blackstrap molasses

Preheat the oven to 350°F (175°C).

Add the almond flour, buckwheat flour, chickpea flour, salt, cinnamon and nutmeg to the bowl of a food processor and pulse a few times to combine. Drizzle in the melted butter, maple syrup, vanilla and molasses and pulse a few more times, until the mixture forms a ball. Remove the dough from the processor and divide it in half. Place one half of the dough between two large pieces of parchment paper. Use a rolling pin to roll the dough out until it is about ⅛ inch (3 mm) thick. Try to keep the thickness even (this will make for even baking).

Remove the top layer of the parchment paper and use a pizza cutter to cut the dough into uniform cracker shapes. There is no need to separate the crackers yet; they will break apart easily after baking! If desired, use a fork to make indents in each cracker. Carefully lift the parchment paper (with the dough still on it) and place it on a baking sheet. Repeat this process with the second ball of dough.

Place the baking sheets side by side in the oven and bake until the edges are lightly browned, 15 to 20 minutes. Cooking times will vary depending on the thickness of your crackers, so start checking your crackers around the 12-minute mark. If the outer crackers start browning faster than the inner crackers, you can remove them with a metal spatula first, then return the pan to the oven to finish baking the rest. Remove the pans from the oven and turn the oven down to 200°F (95°C). When the oven has cooled down, place the trays back in the oven to completely dry out and crisp up the crackers. This will take about 2½ to 3 hours (timing will depend on the thickness of your crackers). You will know the crackers are done when they are crispy and break apart easily.

Store in an airtight container at room temperature for 5 to 7 days.

Duck-Fat Tortilla Chips with Farm-Stand Salsa

Yield: 50 chips and 3 cups (750 g) salsa

Folks! These tortilla chips are AMAZING! They are a fun treat to whip up, and I love that I know exactly what's in them—as opposed to store-bought tortilla chips, which are usually fried in a seed or vegetable oil. These chips are fried in nourishing duck fat, which has a high smoke point and is a healthier option. The only equipment you need for these chips is a large cast-iron pan and a candy thermometer (though you can get by without the thermometer and just test a chip). We love serving these chips with our famous Farm-Stand Salsa. When the tomatoes are cranking at the farm, this salsa is on repeat during the summer months.

Duck-Fat Tortilla Chips

8 corn tortillas (nothing fancy, make sure the ingredients are simply corn)

½ cup (120 g) duck fat (see Note)

Unrefined coarse sea salt

Farm-Stand Salsa

2 cups (298 g) fresh summer tomatoes, chopped (a mix of heirlooms, cherry tomatoes and round reds is wonderful!)

¼ cup (40 g) chopped red onion

2 cloves garlic, minced

1 jalapeño pepper, seeded and minced

2 tbsp (30 ml) fresh lime juice

¼ cup (4 g) finely chopped fresh cilantro

¼ tsp unrefined salt

A grind or two of fresh black pepper

To make the tortilla chips, line a plate with paper towels.

Grab your toddler or favorite kitchen assistant and hand them a pizza cutter. Slice each tortilla in half and then into uniform triangles, creating about six chips per tortilla (depending on the size of your corn tortillas).

In a large cast-iron pan over medium-high heat, melt the duck fat until it reaches about 350°F (175°C). (At this point let your toddler watch from afar, as you don't want hot oil splattering out of the pan onto them!) Distribute the tortillas in a single layer in the cast-iron pan and sprinkle with a little sea salt. Fry the chips for 30 to 45 seconds, then flip the chips. Continue to flip the chips until evenly golden brown and crisp, a total of about 2 minutes. Remove the batch of chips to the paper towel–lined plate to drain. Repeat with the remaining tortillas.

Store chips in a sealed container at room temperature for up to 3 to 5 days.

To make the salsa, add the tomatoes, onion, garlic, jalapeño, lime juice, cilantro, salt and pepper to a food processor and pulse a few times until the mixture is well combined but remains rather chunky. Taste for seasonings and adjust as needed.

Store in an airtight glass container in the fridge for up to 1 week.

Note: Duck fat can be found in most grocery stores, or online.

Energy Balls 3 Ways

I love having these little fruit and nut balls on hand for easy snacking. Pepper loves these so much, and I love throwing them in her lunch box for daycare or having them handy when she is spending the day on the farm with us and needs a little energy boost between meals. I've shared a version of these on my blog and got rave reviews from moms of toddlers, so I knew I had to produce more versions to share in this book. These are reminiscent of a Lärabar, but I love that we're not wasting extra packaging on individual bars, and each batch makes a lot of balls. These store well in the fridge for up to 3 weeks and freeze well for 3 months. Feel free to play around with your own flavor combinations. We're big turmeric–ginger fans, we love cardamom and we can't get enough of the ginger–molasses during the winter months.

Sunshine Balls

Yield: 12 balls

1 cup (120 g) packed dates, pitted and sliced in half

1 cup (146 g) sprouted cashews (hazelnuts, walnuts, macadamia nuts or almonds would also work fine)

½ tsp ground turmeric

½ tsp ground ginger

½ tsp ground cinnamon

Pinch of finely ground black pepper

Pinch of unrefined sea salt

½ tsp pure vanilla extract (optional)

Soak the dates in hot water for 15 minutes. Drain and set aside.

Add the cashews to the bowl of a food processor along with the turmeric, ginger, cinnamon, pepper and salt. Process until a fine meal is achieved, scraping down the sides of the processor as necessary.

Add the drained dates and the vanilla extract (if using) and process until a sticky dough forms. Transfer the mixture to the fridge for about 10 minutes to firm up a bit.

Take tablespoon-sized (15-g) portions of the dough and roll the mixture between your palms into small, uniform balls.

Store in an airtight container in the fridge for up to 2 weeks or freeze for up to 3 months.

Ginger-Molasses Energy Balls

Yield: 12 balls

1 cup (120 g) packed dates, pitted and sliced in half

1 cup (117 g) sprouted walnuts (hazelnuts, cashews, almonds or macadamia nuts would also work, or use a mixture of nuts)

1 tsp ground cinnamon

½ tsp ground ginger

¼ tsp ground allspice

¼ tsp ground nutmeg

Pinch of unrefined sea salt

½ tsp pure vanilla extract (optional)

1 tbsp (15 ml) blackstrap molasses

Soak the dates in hot water for 15 minutes. Drain and set aside.

Add the walnuts to the bowl of a food processor along with the cinnamon, ginger, allspice, nutmeg and salt. Process until a fine meal is achieved, scraping down the sides of the processor as necessary.

Add the drained dates, vanilla extract (if using) and molasses and process until a sticky dough forms. Transfer the mixture to the fridge for about 10 minutes to firm up a bit.

Take tablespoon-sized (15-g) portions of the dough and roll the mixture between your palms into small, uniform balls.

Store in an airtight container in the fridge for up to 2 weeks or freeze for up to 3 months.

Vanilla Cardamom Energy Balls

Yield: 12 balls

---

1 cup (120 g) packed dates, pitted and sliced in half

1 cup (146 g) sprouted cashews (hazelnuts, walnuts, macadamia nuts or almonds would also work fine)

½ tsp ground cardamom

Pinch of unrefined sea salt

½ tsp pure vanilla extract

Soak the dates in hot water for 15 minutes. Drain and set aside.

Add the cashews to the bowl of a food processor along with the cardamom and salt. Process until a fine meal is achieved, scraping down the sides of the processor as necessary.

Add the drained dates and the vanilla extract and process until a sticky dough forms. Transfer the mixture to the fridge for about 10 minutes to firm up a bit.

Take tablespoon-sized (15-g) portions of the dough and roll the mixture between your palms into small, uniform balls.

Store in an airtight container in the fridge for up to 2 weeks or freeze for up to 3 months.

Sprouted Nut & Seed Granola Bars

Yield: 12–18 bars

These nut and seed bars have saved us on many occasions! When we are out and about running errands or on a hike, these tasty bars come in handy as a simple protein-packed snack to have for quick nourishment. Sweetened with fiber-rich dates and bursting with comforting flavors of cardamom and vanilla, these bars are sure to be a new family favorite snack in your household as well! These also pack really well into school lunch boxes and keep for more than a month in the fridge!

½ cup (60 g) Medjool dates, pitted (about 5–6 large dates)

½ cup (120 ml) boiling water

1 cup (117 g) sprouted walnuts

1 cup (146 g) sprouted cashews

½ cup (67 g) sprouted sunflower seeds

1 cup (93 g) unsweetened shredded coconut

3 tbsp (42 g) coconut oil

2 tbsp (32 g) almond butter

2 tsp (10 ml) almond extract

1 tsp ground cardamom

½ tsp unrefined salt

Preheat the oven to 325°F (165°C) and line a 9 x 9–inch (23 x 23–cm) baking pan with parchment paper.

Place the dates in a bowl with the boiling water and let them soak for 10 minutes.

While the dates soak, place the walnuts, cashews, sunflower seeds and coconut into the bowl of a food processor. Process until it becomes a finely ground texture. Pour the mixture into a large bowl and set aside.

Add the dates to the bowl of the food processor along with ¼ cup (60 ml) of the soaking water, the coconut oil, almond butter, almond extract, cardamon and salt. Process until a thick paste forms.

Add the date mixture to the bowl with the dry ingredients and use a wooden spoon to mix it together. Spoon the mixture into the prepared pan. Place another layer of parchment paper on top and press down with your hands firmly to help pack down and evenly distribute the mixture. Remove the top layer of parchment.

Place the granola bars in the oven and bake for 30 to 45 minutes, until golden brown and firm. Remove the pan from the oven and gently lift the parchment paper out of the pan and place on a cooling rack. Let the bars cool for 1 hour (during this time they will firm up even more).

Slice into bars and store at room temperature for up to 7 days or place in the fridge for up to 1 month.

Sweet Treats
& Baked Goods

I read a quote on Instagram a while ago from Emily Ventura, co-author of the book *Sugarproof*, that said, "It's easier to parent kids when they aren't on the sugar roller coaster. And it's easier to parent kids when you aren't on the sugar roller coaster."

This quote totally resonates and, since becoming a mom, I have totally cleaned up my sugar intake because I know when I'm on that sugar high, I get irritable, short and don't feel like the best version of myself. And when the roles are reversed, and I know Pepper has had too much sugar, she is in a total tailspin of highs and lows. So, with that in mind, I wanted to touch on the importance of treats being simply that—treats. Not something we serve often but, when we do, we take special care to make them delicious, memorable and something worth celebrating.

Making treats is also a great opportunity to get your kiddos in the kitchen helping. I have such fond memories of baking with my own mom, and there is something so special about taking a freshly baked cookie out of the oven and clinking glasses of milk and enjoying a homemade treat with the people you love. And because treats are not on the menu often, they feel that much more special when we break out our wooden spoons, measuring cups and whisk. It also helps to share the treats with loved ones or neighbors because food really is a special love language, and sharing it makes it all the sweeter.

All of the recipes that follow are sweetened with dates or maple syrup. The U.S. Centers for Disease Control and Prevention does not recommend sugar (even naturally sweetened sugars like honey or maple syrup) to be added to food for children under the age of 2. For that reason, only serve recipes sweetened with dates (which are considered a whole food) to younger babies and save the ones sweetened with maple syrup until after their second birthday.

I hope these baked goods and sweet treats are recipes that you and your little ones enjoy making together. Hopefully, the memories you create for your family while whipping up some of these treats are ones your kids will carry with them for the rest of their lives. Grab a wooden spoon and your eager-to-help kiddos and enjoy!

Almond Thumbprint Cookies with Cherry–Chia Jam

Yield: 20 cookies

These cookies are divine. They are a lovely cookie to add to your holiday baking list or to simply whip up any time of the year. The recipe calls for using frozen cherries for the jam (we freeze summer cherries specifically for recipes like this!), but you can use fresh cherries as well. The leftover jam tastes great when stirred into oatmeal, spread onto a peanut butter sandwich or smeared over Maple Graham Crackers (page 131). The cookies themselves are lightly sweetened with maple syrup, and the addition of almond extract gives them an extra decadent flavor that just sticks with you. We love these cookies so much, and they are a fun treat to make with your little kitchen helper because making the thumb indent in the cookies is a total thrill for a toddler, and spooning in the jam (and trying their best to get it in the center of the cookie!) is a great activity. The batter is also delicious and, because it does not contain raw eggs, I highly encourage you to let your toddler lick the batter bowl and wooden spoons clean!

Cherry–Chia Jam

2 cups (310 g) pitted frozen cherries

2 tbsp (22 g) chia seeds

1 tsp pure vanilla extract

Preheat the oven to 350°F (175°C). Grease a cookie sheet and set aside.

To prepare the jam, place the frozen cherries in a medium-sized saucepan set over medium-high heat. Heat until the cherries begin to break down a bit. Use a wooden spoon or potato masher (or your immersion blender) to mash the cherries up to your desired consistency. Add the chia seeds and vanilla extract and remove from the heat. Let the mixture sit for 10 minutes to thicken up (it will continue to thicken the longer it sits).

(continued)

Almond Thumbprint Cookies with Cherry–Chia Jam

(continued)

Cookies

2 cups (190 g) blanched almond flour

¼ cup (60 ml) pure maple syrup

¼ cup (60 ml) melted butter

¼ tsp unrefined salt

1 tsp almond extract

While the jam is thickening, make the cookies. In a large mixing bowl, stir the almond flour, maple syrup, butter, salt and almond extract until well combined.

Scoop out tablespoon-sized (15-g) portions of the dough and use your hands to roll each portion into a small ball. Place each ball on the greased cookie sheet, leaving about ½ inch (1.3 cm) of space between each cookie. When all the balls of dough are on the prepared baking sheet, use your thumb to gently indent the center of each cookie (the sides may crack a bit and that's totally okay!). You don't need deep indents, just a light touch of the thumb is good enough!

Fill each indent with a tiny spoonful of the jam (about 1 teaspoon per cookie). Bake in the oven until the cookies are lightly browned and cooked through, 13 to 17 minutes. Baking times will vary depending on the size of your cookies. These cookies will be on the softer side as you remove them from the oven, but they will harden up a bit as they rest.

Serve immediately or store in glass containers in the fridge for up to 7 days or freeze for up to 3 months.

Food for Thought: A few tips for having your little one help you cook. Pre-measure ingredients and place them in small bowls or cups that your child can pour into a saucepan or large baking bowl. This will make things less messy and your little one will have more success navigating ingredients when they're already portioned out. As always, stay close to your child near a hot stove or oven.

Moose Chocolate, aka Chocolate Mousse

Yield: 6 servings
(depending on ages and appetites)

This recipe got its name because, when Pepper was little, she thought chocolate mousse literally meant that a moose eats chocolate. She started to refer to this as "moose chocolate" when she was 2 and the name has stuck. This is one of those sweet treats that I feel really good about serving because of all of the nourishing fats, fiber and antioxidants provided by the cacao powder. We sometimes add "toppings" to our moose chocolate in the form of shredded coconut, crushed nuts and a drizzle of almond butter. Go wild!

¾ cup (90 g) packed Medjool dates, pitted (about 6 dates)

½ cup (120 ml) boiling water

3 average-sized ripe avocados, pitted

1½ tsp (8 ml) vanilla extract

4 tbsp (20 g) raw cacao powder

1 tsp ground cinnamon

Pinch of unrefined sea salt

Place the dates in a bowl and cover with the boiling water. Soak for 30 minutes.

Add the dates and their soaking water to the bowl of a food processor. Process until a paste forms. Add the avocados, vanilla, cacao powder, cinnamon and salt. Process until smooth.

Store in an airtight glass container in the fridge for up to 4 days. Serve chilled.

Flourless Carrot Cake Brownies

Yield: 12 brownies

One of my favorite desserts as a little kid was carrot cake cupcakes. As an adult, I love seeing that my daughter shares my love for carrot cake. These brownies are amazing. They are made with simple ingredients, sweetened with dates only, and provide a balance of fat, fiber and a little protein for a delightful little treat that won't spike blood sugar.

5 large Medjool dates, pitted

½ cup (120 ml) boiling water

¾ cup (194 g) almond butter (sprouted if possible, see Note)

1 tsp vanilla extract

1 tsp cinnamon

½ tsp ground ginger

¼ tsp ground nutmeg

¼ tsp unrefined salt

Pinch of ground cloves

1 cup (110 g) shredded carrots

1 cup (93 g) shredded coconut

¾ tsp baking soda

1 egg, whisked

Preheat the oven to 350°F (175°C). Grease an 8 x 8–inch (20 x 20–cm) baking dish with a healthy cooking fat (coconut oil, ghee or butter) and set aside.

Soak the dates in the boiling water for 10 minutes to soften. Then place the dates, along with the soaking water, in a food processor and process until a smooth paste forms (a few clumps are fine).

In a large bowl, combine the processed dates, almond butter, vanilla, cinnamon, ginger, nutmeg, salt, cloves, carrots, coconut, baking soda and egg and whisk until smooth. Spread the mixture into the prepared baking pan and bake in the oven until cooked through, 25 to 30 minutes or until a toothpick comes out almost clean when inserted in the center of a brownie. Cooking times will vary depending on the texture of your almond butter.

Note: I like the sprouted almond butter from Philosopher Foods. Not only is it organic but it is the only certified "glyphosate residue free" nut butter on the market. Glyphosate is the most heavily used herbicide in agriculture, and it can contaminate nearby crops that haven't been sprayed with it. This certification ensures that no trace of the chemical is present.

Date, Coconut & Chocolate Freezer Cookies

Yield: 12 cookies

These little cookies could not be easier to whip up, and they are really fun to make with your toddler. Between rolling the dough, flattening it with the palm of your hand and then using a straw to poke littles holes, it's the best activity! Pepper loves making these, and we love eating them together with a cup of milk for a tasty little afternoon treat.

1 cup + 1 tbsp (99 g) unsweetened shredded coconut, divided

1 cup (120 g) Medjool dates, pitted (about 10 large dates)

1 tsp ground cinnamon

¼ tsp unrefined salt

3 tbsp (45 ml) melted coconut oil

3 tbsp (15 g) cacao powder

1–2 tsp (5–10 ml) maple syrup

½ tsp vanilla extract

Line a baking sheet with parchment paper; set aside.

In a large, dry cast-iron skillet over medium heat, lightly toast the 1 cup (93 g) of coconut, using a wooden spoon to mix it around every so often. Keep a close eye on the coconut, as you don't want it to burn. Remove the pan from the heat.

Place the dates, toasted coconut, cinnamon and salt in a food processor. Process until a dough ball forms. Remove the mixture from the processor and take 1-inch (2.5-cm)-sized portions of the dough and roll into a ball. Place each ball on the parchment-lined baking sheet and then lightly flatten into a "cookie" shape with your palm. Use a straw to poke holes in each cookie, lightly moving the straw around to get a wider hole if needed. You may need to reshape your cookie a bit after doing this. Place the cookies in the freezer for 10 minutes to firm up a bit.

While the cookies are in the freezer, in a medium bowl, whisk the coconut oil, cacao powder, maple syrup and vanilla extract until well combined. Remove the cookies from the freezer and dip each cookie into the glaze. Then drizzle the remainder of the glaze on top of each cookie and sprinkle with the remaining 1 tablespoon (6 g) of coconut. Place the cookies back in the freezer for 15 minutes so the chocolate can harden.

Store the cookies in an airtight glass container in the freezer for up to 3 months. These taste best when removed from the freezer and left to sit for 3 to 5 minutes before eating.

Pumpkin Molasses Oat Muffins

Yield: 12 muffins

These are a delicious and festive muffin for the holidays or simply a bright spot on a dreary winter day. They are chock full of flavor and are minimally sweet with a lovely combination of spices. As an ode to the fall harvest of hazelnuts in Oregon, we chose to use hazelnut flour in these muffins, but almond flour is a perfect substitute. I love the addition of the blackstrap molasses for its rich flavor and health benefits. Molasses is a wonderful sweetener to add to baked goods for children because it is high in iron and has a well-balanced mineral content.

1¼ cups (150 g) sprouted oat flour (see Note on page 41)

1¼ cups (120 g) hazelnut or almond flour (or sunflower seed flour for a nut-free version)

1 tsp baking soda

½ tsp unrefined salt

1 tsp ground ginger

1 tsp ground cinnamon

¼ tsp ground nutmeg

2 room-temperature eggs, whisked

½ cup (120 ml) melted butter or coconut oil

¼ cup (60 ml) pure maple syrup

¼ cup (60 ml) blackstrap molasses

1 tsp vanilla extract

1 cup (246 g) roasted and mashed pumpkin, butternut or Hubbard squash (see Note)

Preheat the oven to 350°F (175°C). Line a standard muffin tin with parchment paper muffin liners and set aside.

In a large mixing bowl, combine the oat flour, hazelnut flour, baking soda, salt, ginger, cinnamon and nutmeg. In a medium-sized bowl, stir together the eggs, butter, maple syrup, molasses and vanilla extract. Pour the wet ingredients into the bowl with the flour and mix well. Stir in the roasted pumpkin until evenly combined (a few lumps is okay!).

Pour the batter into the prepared muffin tin and bake in the oven until a toothpick comes out clean when inserted into the center of a muffin, 18 to 22 minutes. Start checking around the 18-minute mark.

Store the muffins in an airtight container at room temperature for 1 day, in the fridge for up to 5 days, or freeze for up to 3 months.

Note: I prefer roasting and mashing/pureeing my own squash instead of using canned pumpkin, as the canned pumpkin tends to be more watery and less flavorful. To roast, simply slice whatever squash variety you are using in half. Scoop out the seeds and place cut-side down on a rimmed baking sheet. Drizzle in ¼ cup (60 ml) of water and roast at 350°F (175°C) until fork tender, about 45 minutes, depending on your squash. Use a potato masher to mash the squash before storing (or for a smoother consistency you can blend the roasted squash in a blender). Use leftovers for Pumpkin Chili (page 101), Pumpkin Meatballs (page 54) or Curry Pumpkin Soft Scrambled Eggs (page 51).

Little Remedies

It's inevitable that, at some point or another, our little ones will come down with an illness or just be struggling with some discomfort. And while speaking with your doctor should be your first step if you are concerned about anything, I'm sharing some of my go-to little remedies for basic illness. I hope some of these can help soothe your little one when they're not feeling like themselves.

Prune Puree (for Constipation)

Yield: 8–10 servings

This recipe makes a decent amount because I think you'll find it useful to have on hand. It's easy to freeze in ice cube trays and you can just pop one out when needed and let it defrost in the refrigerator. We served this almost daily when Pepper first started solids because she really struggled with constipation, and this was the only thing that helped! It tastes great, too, and I loved adding a little spoonful to my morning cup of oatmeal. It helps to keep everyone regular!

1 cup (174 g) dried prunes

1 small pear, peeled, cored and chopped

Dash of cinnamon

1 tbsp (14 g) unsalted butter, coconut oil or ghee

Add the prunes and pear to a saucepan and cover with water. Bring to a boil. Reduce the heat and simmer until the prunes and pear have softened, about 5 minutes. Drain.

When cool enough to handle, add the cooked fruit to a food processor or blender along with the cinnamon and butter and puree.

Store in an airtight container in the refrigerator for 4 days or freeze for up to 3 months.

Bone Broth (for Basic Illness)

Yield: 2 quarts (1.9 L)

There really is nothing more soothing than sipping a cup of warm broth when you aren't feeling well, and the same goes for our kiddos. Nourishing bone broth is an incredible way to get important minerals into our little ones when their appetites are down and they are feeling crummy. Broth freezes well and is easy to thaw. I like to double or triple this recipe when I have a lot of bones to use up from a few weeks' worth of cooking different meats. Feel free to use this recipe as a guide and adjust as needed.

4 lb (1.8 kg) bones (chicken, beef, turkey, pork, lamb or whatever you've got on hand)

4 qt (3.8 L) water

2 tbsp (30 ml) apple cider vinegar

Preheat the oven to 400°F (205°C).

Place the bones in a colander and rinse them under cold water. Pat them dry with a dish towel and then place the bones in a single layer on a rimmed baking sheet or two. Roast until they are lightly browned, about 30 minutes.

Add the bones to a large stockpot or Dutch oven. Add the water and the vinegar and stir to combine. Cover the pot and let it sit for 30 minutes (this allows the vinegar to extract nutrients from the bones).

Bring the water to a low boil over high heat. Reduce the heat to low, cover the pot and simmer for 12 to 24 hours. Check the pot occasionally to skim off any foam from the surface and to add more water as necessary.

Strain the broth and discard the bones. Divide the broth between mason jars and keep it in the fridge for 1 week or the freezer for up to 6 months.

Electrolyte Drink (for Dehydration)

Yield: 1 pint (473 ml)

It's important to keep our little ones hydrated when they aren't feeling well. Babies under the age of 1 should stick to breastfeeding as their primary source of hydration and nourishment when they are ill. For babies over 1, this is a nice drink to offer when they are under the weather.

2 cups (480 ml) filtered water

Juice of half a lemon

1 tsp pure maple syrup

Pinch of unrefined salt

Mix the water, lemon juice, maple syrup and salt and keep in a large jar or pitcher. Serve ½ cup (120 ml) at a time or as needed for your little one.

Evening Chamomile Tea (for Winding Down)

Yield: 1 serving

No one has more on their to-do list than a toddler at bedtime! Enter this calming chamomile tea. Chamomile is a wonderful pantry staple if you have little ones. It contains antioxidants and can help regulate sleep, aid in digestion and reduce stress. As part of an evening ritual, we like to brew up some tea and serve it with a splash of milk or cream. Pepper has her own special mug, which makes her even more excited to settle down for the evening with her calming tea.

1 tsp loose-leaf chamomile

½ cup (120 ml) hot water

Whole milk or cream (for serving)

Steep the chamomile in hot water for 8 to 10 minutes. Strain the tea and let the tea cool down for 15 minutes. Test the temperature and, when lukewarm, add the milk or cream to taste and serve your toddler in their favorite special mug. Good luck with bedtime! I'm with you in spirit.

Acknowledgments

My deepest gratitude to my husband, Taylor, for always supporting me and continuously easing the burden with every project I take on. The girls and I are so lucky to have you as our rock.

Thank you also to:

My agent, Jenny Stephens, for all your guidance and support for the past 7 years! Three cookbooks later and I couldn't imagine this wild ride without you. You're simply the best.

The entire team at Page Street Publishing. Thank you for believing in this book and taking my project on! I am so lucky to have landed in your welcoming hands.

Jessica Cassidy, thank you for helping me get my initial proposal underway. I honestly could not have done this without you.

Kelly Turso, where do I begin? Thank you for being my friend (first and foremost) and for taking all the farm photographs in this book. You are such a talent!

Ashley Marti, girl! Your eye for style is top notch. Three books later and you continue to help make these books so beautiful.

My sister-in-law Charlotte Boylan, thank you for testing so many of the recipes in this book and for being "my person" when it comes to all things motherhood. I couldn't imagine this chapter of my life without you in it.

My mom, for all your support and recipe testing over the years. Thank you for always being honest and encouraging.

To my midwives, Charli, Sarah and Emily. You were my gateway into the world of unconventional care and gave me the courage to start advocating for my health and the health of my unborn babies. Now that they are earth side, there is no stopping me. Thank you for helping to light my fire!

To all my blog readers and Instagram community. This book would never have happened if it weren't for all of you.

Last and certainly not least, thank you to all the farmers out there who feed us all.

Before We Eat
by Pat Brisson

As we sit around this table let's give thanks as we are able, to all the folks we'll never meet who helped provide this food we eat.

They plowed the ground and planted seeds,

Tended fields, removed the weeds.

They picked the food at harvest time, working in the heat and grime.

They grazed the cattle, fed the sows, gathered eggs, and milked the cows.

They fished from boats out on the seas; raised wheat and nuts and honeybees.

Thank the ones who packed the crates, sorted boxes, checked the weights.

Thank the drivers on the roads in their trucks with heavy loads.

And all the clerks at all the stores who did the grocery-selling chores.

Thank the ones who bought this food, the ones who teach me gratitude.

Sitting at this meal we share, we are grateful and aware, sending thanks upon the air . . .

To those workers . . . everywhere.

About the Author

Andrea Bemis is the author of *Dishing Up the Dirt* and *Local Dirt*. Both cookbooks are centered around farm-to-table cooking. She lives and works on her family farm, Tumbleweed Farm, with her husband, Taylor, and their two daughters, Pepper and Maize. In addition to managing the farm, she and her husband run a CSA program that feeds more than 130 families, and they sell their vegetables at their local farmers' market and restaurants in their community. When she isn't busy digging her hands in the dirt, she is often in her kitchen with her family dishing up meals and making a mess. You can find her on Instagram @andreabemis.

Index